M000288306

Don't You Fall Now

a memoir

CLAUDIA LOVE MAIR

Don't You Fall Now

a memoir

CLAUDIA LOVE MAIR

New Season
BOOKS AND MEDIA

DON'T YOU FALL NOW
@2018 by Claudia Love Mair

ISBN: 978-0-692-10857-4

NewSeason Books and Media
PO Box 1403
Havertown, PA 19083
www.newseasonbooks.com
newseasonbooks@gmail.com

Cover Design: Annie Crandell

All rights reserved. No part of this book may be reproduced in any form or by any means including electronic, mechanical or photocopying or stored in a retrieval system without permission in writing from the publisher except by a reviewer who may quote brief passages to be included in a review.

Author's Note

When patients are admitted into a behavioral health facility, their privacy is protected. Two adolescents' stories were vital to me and to this memoir. I have changed the names of these brave youths, as well as other identifying features, to ensure their private pain remains private. I am grateful for how their lives intersected with mine when we were all so fragile.

For Kamau: the bravest man I know.

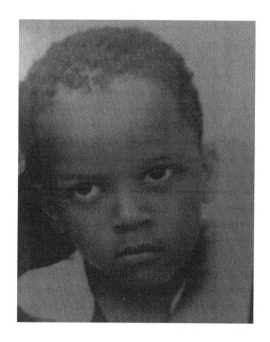

"Don't you fall now —
For I'se still goin', honey,
I'se still climbin',
And life for me ain't been no crystal stair."

Langston Hughes, Mother to Son

Part One

1
April 27, 2012

BAM! BAM! BAM! BAM! The voice in my head is my mama's: *They knockin' like the po-lice!*

"ZZ, help me," I say.

My agile 'tween daughter leaps out of my bed and rushes into the painting studio that was once our living room. I hobble behind her, numb feet slapping against the yellow concrete floor, my heart thumping like a talking drum.

She pulls the sheers aside and peers out. Confirms what I already know. "Mom, it's the police."

Kamau. It's got to be. My youngest son. He's supposed to be at his brother's. I swing the door open to a pair of officers. The young, uniformed one appears earnest and sincere. The older, bald, plainclothes cop somber.

The elder of the two does the talking. "I'm Detective Franz with Lexington Police Homicide, and this is officer blah, blah, blah . . . Are you Kamau Burney's mother?"

Homicide? The police were here two months ago to the day about my boy, but not a homicide detective. I hold my arms. His news will kill me.

"Yes, I am."

"There's been an accident. He fell off a building."

Oh, God. I think I'm going to die right this instance.

"He's okay. He's at the hospital right now."

"He's okay?"

"Yes, ma'am. He's in intensive care."

Relief washes over me, yet a fleeting image of Kamau flying wingless toward the street, skyscrapers static in the background drifts to mind. He's falling, like jumpers from the burning Twin

Towers. Falling, like a ragged brown leaf in the wind, but I can't picture him hitting the ground.

"I think it was from Rupp Arena," the man says.

I stare at Detective Franz like he's spoken some archaic form of English I can barely comprehend. The Rupp, a huge convention center downtown, flashes before me. I feel sick to my stomach.

"Come in," I say. I step aside and let the officers into the studio. I teach painting to women in my spare time. I'm trying to make a business of it, but it's going slowly. The officers take in my creative space.

A wall the color of young grass greets the policeman. My friend, novelist and artist Lisa Samson, has chalked the words "Good Medicine Expressive Arts Studio" below a gilded framed print of Our Lady of Guadalupe. Three black chalkboard walls surround the green, decorated with graffiti applied by some of my painting students but mostly my own kids — Abbie, Kamau, Nia, and ZZ. A tiny sofa sits in the back of the room. I ask the men if they would like to have a seat. They refuse, so ZZ and I ease onto the small, black canvas cushions.

"Tell me about your son's state of mind?" Detective Franz fires at me.

His state of mind? How much time do you have?

2
The Bus: *January 2012*

Kamau bursts into my bedroom full of a wild energy I wish I had. I'm lying in bed like I do much of the time in winter, like many of us seasonally affective-disordered depressives do.

"Mom," he says, springing onto my bed like he's seven instead of seventeen. "You gotta hear what happened to me on the bus today. It was awesome!"

I slink upward, resting on my elbows. "What happened on the bus?"

His arms gesture his enthusiasm. "I could read everyone's mind, and all their thoughts revolved around me. I was the sun, and they orbited around me."

"Really?"

I do a quick inventory of his most recent reading material, as if this will explain what he said. He's reading Nietzsche, anarchist, and paranormal stuff. I recall seeing some Eastern mysticism. It's almost the same stuff that would have been found in my book bag when I was his age. Kamau goes on and on about being the center of the Lextran, our local bus service, universe.

"Did anything else happen?" I ask, concern knotting in my belly. I sit up straight, and shield my chest with the comforter.

"I went to Kroger, and I could read everyone's mind in there, too."

"What were they thinking about?"

"They were thinking about *me*," he says, as if it's the most obvious thing in the world.

"They were *all* thinking about you? Like, *everybody*?"

He nods like a bobble head. "Yeah, Mom." He beams. "I felt like *God*."

Kamau has always been a little weird. He's the kid with the quirky sense of humor who never goes for the obvious joke. When he was in middle school, we talked nonsense to each other, cackling at the absurdity of our speech. Kamau is silly in the best way, a likeable kid who never met a stranger.

He seems so very Kamau right now: same bouncy energy and short, springy, dreadlocks sprouting from his head: same happy, goofball manner and gap-toothed smile.

"Did anything else happen?"

He shook his head. "Nah, but that was *amaaazing!*"

Schizophrenia, bipolar disorder, and addictions run in our family, knocking off aunts, uncles, cousins, and siblings like a car careening out of control. The casualties "crazy" leaves behind stretch across generations.

I take a long look at my boy, inhale then exhale hard. I've never told him this. I've rarely told anyone. "When I was twenty-one-years-old, I thought I was going to disappear."

"Yeah?" He sits on the bed next to me.

"It seemed so real, Kamau. I mean, I knew in the back of my mind that people don't up and vanish, but the idea seized me. It wouldn't let me go."

He nods, his serious expression mirroring my own.

"That was my first and only psychotic break, and I didn't recognize it for what it was for years. I had little help, just a boyfriend who was familiar with the mental health system. My family didn't even know I was sick."

Kamau listened, head cocked, big brown eyes fixed on mine.

"At the time I practiced yoga and steeped myself in the teachings of Eastern religions and New Age spiritual masters. My reading resembled yours, if you take away Nietzsche and add Kabir and Rumi. I don't think the stuff I learned led to my illness, but I'm pretty sure it fueled my delusion. Anything can."

"You think I had a delusion?" He doesn't seem offended, just curious. "You think I'm crazy, Ma?"

I shrug. "What is crazy? That's not a clinical term, and we throw it around—I do it myself—when we're talking about people who are really sick."

"I'm not sick."

"Sweetie, what you're saying is familiar."

The spring I thought I would disappear? I was *so* creative. I did everything: painted, wrote pages and pages of poetry and short stories, acted. I would stay up all night, my thoughts soaring.

"Kamau, I felt like a supernova, with nothing more to achieve but oneness with God. Poof! I'd just disappear. Nothing could sway me from this idea, even though a part of me knew that kind of thing didn't really happen, except to very special people. Chosen people, and I thought maybe I was chosen. You know?"

He nods again, and I'm certain he knows.

"I'm bipolar. My father was bipolar. I have two aunts who are schizophrenic. I told myself that I would watch for any signs of mental illness in my kids."

"Mom, we're all right."

"I'm not so sure you are, bud. Do you ever feel like you've got too many thoughts all at once, fighting to be thought about, and you want to think them all, but they're going too fast?"

He looks at me, as trusting as an infant. "Yeah."

"Baby," I say, "it's possible that you're bipolar, and you're having a manic episode."

He lies back on my bed, staring at the ceiling. We don't say anything for a while. A few minutes later, I tell Kamau all I know about bipolar disorder, how it can make you feel like you've touched heaven, right before it plunges you into hell. I tell him how seductive manic states are, how they can make you feel invincible. It's hard to tell what's safe when you're that way because everything feels safe. I tell him the huge stuff happening in his head may feel real, but the feeling doesn't make it so.

I think, like me, Kamau will ride the big waves of bliss. A budding filmmaker, he'll make his films and write like a fiend, then deal with the crushing ebb of depression by dragging himself back to a safe shore: me. I will be there to hold his hand as he lies on the sofa spent, and I'll remind him to shower, change his clothes, and brush his teeth.

When it becomes too much, I'll take him to a kind, understanding psychiatrist for medicine. That's how I survived bipolar disorder and lived. I raised a family. I taught myself the number one rule: don't hurt Claudia. I will teach Kamau his own rule of life. He won't hurt himself, and we will be all right. That's what I thought. I was wrong.

3
Psychological Profile

Now, Detective Franz fires questions at me in my little studio. He's crafting a psychological profile, to help him determine what would make Kamau do such a thing. I understand this police business, and try to cooperate.

"Tell me about your son's state of mind?"

"I think he's been becoming manic. He's bipolar, with psychotic features. He's been non-compliant with his medicines, but I made him get back on them today. I could tell he was getting sick again." I'm tapping my foot. Taptaptaptaptaptaptap.

That very morning Kamau talked about following the birds, listening to their messages. I don't tell the officers this.

"Have there been any stressors in his life?"

"He broke up with a girlfriend, and he's having a hard time with it, and he hasn't been able to deal with high school. He was trying to complete his courses online, but now he has too much trouble focusing. I took him to the Fayette County Public School's administration building today to drop out so he can get his GED, but he ended up changing his mind and is going to try it again."

I know I'm rambling, but can't stop. My pitch soars upward at the end of every statement. "He went for a walk after that, and then said he was going to his brother's." Tap,tap,tap,tap,tap,tap.

"What's his brother's name and number?"

"Lumumba Bandele, but his phone is disconnected. That's why I wasn't concerned when Kamau didn't call to let me know he was there."

"Any other stressors?"

"I don't know. I mean, his relationship with his friends is a little strained. He hasn't been himself lately." I resist the urge to use clinical terms like "delusions" or "grandiosity."

"Has he mentioned wanting to hurt himself?"

"No," I shake my head almost violently.

"Does he use drugs or alcohol?"

"He smokes a little weed." *God, I hope it's only that.*

I know what all these questions are, but I don't have time for this right now. I stand abruptly.

"Do you know if anyone was with him tonight?" says Officer Franz.

I am done talking. "I need to go to my boy."

The two officers step back like I'm too imposing of a figure to get in the way of.

"Would you like for me to take you?" Detective Franz offers.

"No," I snap. I have the strange idea that if I get into his car, he'll know I don't have car insurance, a broke person's irrational fear. "I'll drive myself."

"Are you sure?" he asks as I'm heading out the door. I see that I'm in my pajamas and turn back. Thoughts swirl around in my head like they're swept up in a funnel cloud as I try to figure out what I need to do next.

"I have to call his dad."

ZZ hands me the landline. No sooner than she gives me the receiver, she hurries to my bedroom to root around for clothes for me. The two policemen stand like sentries in my home studio, waiting.

Ken answers on the second ring. His "hello" is terse and weary.

"Kamau fell from a building."

He groans as if he felt the impact himself.

"I'm headed to the hospital. I'll talk to you when I find out anything." I thrust the phone back at ZZ, slide the clothes she hands me over my pajamas, snatch my keys and purse up from beside the little sofa, and scramble to the hospital, the two cops trailing behind me.

4

Drive

April boasts unseasonably warm temperatures on this gorgeous night in the Bluegrass. My silver Chevy Cavalier slides seamlessly through the velvet comfort of the night. Horror threatens to rise like bile to my throat, but I focus on what's outside of me. Main Street revelers stagger toward campus, predictably loud and obnoxious. I slow to a crawl as a clutch of students, whoop and whistle across my path.

How can they be so happy, ripping and running up and down the street? My child is lying in a hospital bed. God only knows what's going to happen to him. How can life just go on, oblivious to his suffering?

I slide my fingers through my raggedy afro. Again, I see Kamau falling, like a rag doll tossed out of a window. But he isn't that. He's my baby. *Oh, God.* As I drive, my hands grip the steering wheel, and my body rocks my prayer, back and forth, back and forth. *OhGodohGodohGod.*

***

I arrive at UK HealthCare's Albert B. Chandler Hospital looking certifiable. No makeup. My hair a rough tangle of coarse curls, black pajamas peeking from under the shirt and jeans I threw on. I'm wild-eyed and desperate to get to Kamau, forgetting to push the button while I wait for the elevator.

I pace. Lean against the wall. Tap my foot. Everything escapes me, the fact that it's been minutes, but I'm still waiting on the elevator, the pattern of the carpet, the color on the surfaces of things, people passing in the hall. It's all I can do not to wail and thrash so I can arrive at the ICU without the need for four-point restraints. *Oh, God. Please, let him be okay.*

5

Good Grief

When I reach Kamau's room, I step inside like I'm an apparition, watching. So many people crowd around him. They're busy. I can't tell what they're doing. I can only see Kamau's bare legs, lying still beneath a white sheet.

A young woman steps beside me. She's pretty and dark-haired, efficient, but kind. She wears blue scrubs.

"Are you the mom?"

I nod.

"I'm his nurse, Charlie Brown."

Good grief!

"He's a little miracle," she says. "Do you want to see him?"

I'm not sure I do.

Charlie Brown urges me toward the gurney with a decisive nod. I follow her, my steps heavy with dread.

"His mom is here," she says above the buzz of the room. People spread out like she's Moses, parting a sea of lab coats, and I finally see my boy in fragments.

His hand, the long, tapered musician fingers torn and bloody. Abrasions chart a map of pain across his knuckles. I envision his hand when it hit the ground and ripped open his flesh. I see it bounce, his wrist slack.

Kamau's torso is bare, his clavicle swollen and bluing. Broken. A white, plastic cervical collar circles his fractured neck. His head sits erect within it.

I brace myself to look at his face.

Oh. My boy.

Kamau's beautiful face looks unnaturally flat. It spills around the cervical collar, his nose, lips, and eyes distorted. A scarlet opening splits a path across his forehead.

He does not look like my son.

He does not look like Kamau.

This is not my boy.

I open my mouth to scream, but no sound comes out.

"His face is broken," Charlie says. "Every bone. It's like a jigsaw puzzle."

I rock back on my heels. *Oh, sweet Jesus.*

The team has to finish its work. Charlie Brown gently pulls me away. I follow her, docile and obedient. Then I'm in standing by the door again, watching the hurried movements of medical professionals, my mouth still slack. The scream finally comes out as words.

"I have to go to sleep!" I yell. "I have fibromyalgia. I have to sleep. If I don't go to sleep I'm going to get sick." I hold on to my arms, frantic. "I have to go to sleep."

She ushers me out into the hallway, rubbing my shoulders. The sweet nurse speaks in soothing tones. "We'll take care of him. Go home, and we'll see you when you get back."

I speed walk down the hall, fumble for the elevator buttons, and thrust myself inside the open doors. Hold my arms. Rock back and forth. Run to my car full tilt. I speed out of the parking lot, grateful there's no attendant to have to stop for. Flying down Limestone Street, I can't see I'm crying so hard. Sounds I have never made before or since burst out of my body in wave after a wave of unrelenting sobs. If I never believed in angels before, I do this night. Unseen hands guide me safely home.

I understand now why the detective offered to drive me.

6

Stink: *January 2012*

"Mom, Kamau stinks." A frequent complaint from my girls. This time it's Abbie, his older sister pushing me to do something.

I call Kamau into my bedroom and gently ask him to take a shower.

"I already took one, Mom," he says, giving Abbie the side-eye. His ripe aroma indicates he needs another.

"Take a shower, kid," I insist in the mom voice my children know means business. "Don't forget to put on deodorant and change your clothes."

I follow as he trudges into his bedroom, picks up clothing from a pile sprawled across a chair, and sniffs them one by one. Kamau always cleans himself up when asked, but he has to be reminded, sometimes multiple times, and on his own, he's prone to forget a step: the deodorant, or the fresh T-shirt. Soon he reeks again. An odor reminiscent of decaying onions fills the house, and his sisters complain bitterly. The cycle repeats itself for most of the month.

7

Walks

Sometimes, when it's late, and the girls have gone off to their computers, or to watch television, Kamau leaves the house. The hour that he returns grows later and later as the days pass. My anxiety multiplies like weeds.

"Where are you going, Kamau?" I ask one time as his hand reaches for the doorknob.

"Just out for a walk."

"It's eleven o'clock."

At his age, I took walks in the middle of the endless, sleepless nights, none of my family the wiser. I felt *so much* back then, the rich darkness, palpable, the cool air on my skin, alive, the chattering stories in my imagination of the people closed up, safe inside their houses kept me company as I passed them on the street. I felt the brightness of the stars like strobe lights on a dance floor. Sometimes, I'd wonder if I would be murdered, a young woman alone, just walking. I'd craft elaborate deaths in my head, and keep going.

Kamau and I are so much alike, our sicknesses parallel, but he's a young Black male, and the streets are perilous to him. His friends are a tribe of strapping boys, as sweet-tempered as Kamau. They are smart, funny, fearless, creative, and worrisome. They are also White. I've told Kamau that if anything happens while they are out, the justice system would be against him, not the White kids. He is like them, yes, in all the ways that count in the eyes of God and good people, but in a still alarmingly racist society, he is different. He is the feared and dreaded Black Man.

He doesn't get it. Kamau is one of the kindest people I've ever known. My warnings bounce off him like rubber bands he can hardly feel. The world I speak of isn't the world he knows. His father and I sacrificed to create an unsegregated life for our children, unlike the society we grew up in. Our multicultural dream renders him clueless of how harsh the world can be for those of us with brown bodies.

"What do you do while you're out?"

He shrugs. "I just walk. I follow the birds. I'm like Adam, the first man."

Kamau talks a lot about God these days.

Is he in the middle of a religious conversion? I wonder, and I don't feel as anxious about his newfound zeal as I did when he was a fifteen-year-old agnostic. But his talk of God seems odd, cryptic, a threadbare crazy quilt of East, West, and musing that are uniquely Kamau's. I try hard not to judge him. When he tells me that he feels like he's the son of God, but doesn't think he's Jesus. I'm relieved.

Aren't we all the sons of God, I tell myself. *This is okay.*

Nature speaks to him, he tells me.

That's Biblical. God speaks through nature, and Kamau is learning to listen to God's voice that way.

His burgeoning conversion is nothing like my own teenaged born-again experience was. There are no revival meetings. No hallelujahs or amens. No sweeping, weepy, emotional, spiritual manifestations. No frequent church services or youth groups, and no support for his new convictions, except for my puzzled, reluctant acceptance.

As time goes by in the short days of February, his stories become more bizarre. He tells me about the Sun God, Ra. How he's pretty sure he's going to lose his left eye to him. That Ra will create soldiers. He will use Kamau's left eye to watch the goings on of men. There will be a war.

His friends begin to show concern for the things he's saying. Kamau tells them he wants to create an army and rule the United States. His girlfriend will reign with him. He tells me this, too, and I think of myself, the girl who was going to disappear, how the thought came, resided, but eventually passed, unaddressed by anyone but my boyfriend, who listened sympathetically.

"Awww," I remember my boyfriend, David, cooing to me so many years ago. "My babe is going to disappear." His gentleness comforted me. But a few days later, I turned into a storm. Unreasonably angry, the thinnest of provocations a catalyst, I tried to throw myself out of his speeding car. David drove me, with one hand on the steering wheel, and the other holding me, straight to a therapist's office. This kid, not twenty-one-years old, with his own mental health problems, took care of me. He told the intake worker I tried to kill myself. All I knew was that my feelings were suddenly jumbled, a tangle of complicated, ambushing emotions I didn't know how to stop.

All. That. Feeling.

Now I watch my son, a storm himself, push his way out the door for a walk that's much too late in the dark winter night for my comfort, but too early, according to the clock, for me to complain about. He is, after all, almost eighteen years old.

I wonder when his meandering is going to become dangerous. I spend my days worrying about him waiting for a sign that now, today, is the day when I *must* take him to the psychiatric hospital.

I need something unmistakable to happen. I don't believe odd thinking and poor hygiene is enough.

The thought of what I believe is Kamau's first bipolar episode consumes me. Soon, I don't watch for my own signs of mental illness. My thoughts are beginning to scatter like marbles on a hard floor, and I find it more difficult to gather them.

8

From the Police Report:
February 27, 2012

Juvenile Complaint

*I*n the interest of Kamau Burney, a child, the affiant says that in Fayette County, the above-named juvenile committed the act of INDECENT EXPOSURE, 2ND DEGREE. Affiant's grounds of belief are that on 2/27/2012, listed juvenile did intentionally expose his genitals under circumstances that in which he knows or should know that his contact is likely to cause affront or alarm to others. The officer states he was dispatched to LEXMARK in reference to the above juvenile running around the property while naked. This officer states that when he made contact with the juvenile, he stated, "It's okay to be naked."

9

February 27, 2012

Morning. The incessant pounding at my door startles me awake. Aziza, asleep beside me, bolts upright, but I remain curled into myself, my heart pounding hard enough for me to feel my pulse in my throat. I try to unfold my stiff limbs while Aziza scurries out of the bedroom and into the studio.

"Mom, it's the police," I hear her say.

I will my arms and legs to move, and push through pain and a haze of sleep. Trudge through the hallway and toward the cop at the door waiting for us to open up. I do a quick inventory. Abbie has always been a late sleeper. I know she's snoozing away in her room. I saw Nia off to school at 7:30 a.m. Kamau is in his room. All of us are safe.

I swing the door open. The policeman's sober expression confuses me.

"Are you Kamau Burney's mother?"

"Yes?"

"Did you know your son Kamau was walking around on Lexmark's property naked?"

My stunned expression is answer enough, but I shake my head, as if the gesture can dislodge the image from my mind.

"He said it's okay to be naked. Is this something he does?" He glares at me, as if this is something I taught him myself.

"No!" I say, still shaking my head. "He's never done anything like that to my knowledge."

An encounter with the police can go so very wrong for Black men. Did they hurt him? *Oh, God.*

"Is he okay?" Would he even tell me the truth? The fact that this policeman is Black is only a small comfort.

"He's fine. His blood pressure was high, and he's cold, but he's fine. If you follow me, we can go to the hospital they're taking him to."

I'm wearing an oversized, black Norma Kamali button down shirt, and little else. My mind is a whirlwind of thoughts, and modesty isn't my greatest concern, but I can't leave the house dressed like that. I grab the house phone and dial Kamau's dad. When I reach him, I exhale the story out in a single breath: "The police found Kamau wandering around naked. I'm going to the hospital now." I thrust the receiver at the officer. "Can you explain to his father what happened?"

The officer takes the phone, and I hurry to put on the first pair of pants I can find. I yank on mismatched socks and slide my feet into my cowgirl boots, my thoughts tossed about as if an agitator churned them around in my head.

One thing is clear to me, I have to get to my baby as fast as I can.

10

From the Police Report: Resisting Arrest

*A*ffiant's grounds of belief are that on 02/27/2012, the listed juvenile intentionally attempted to prevent this Officer, who was acting under his official authority, from effecting an arrest by using force. This officer states that when he attempted to gain control of the above juvenile, the juvenile began to resist arrest by jerking and pulling away from the officer.

11

An Unmistakable Sign

The policeman and I arrive at Good Samaritan Hospital, where the officer escorts me to the emergency room. When we're buzzed back beyond the waiting area, he takes me to my son.

He pulls the curtain skirting the area. Kamau lies on a narrow gurney, trembling in his pale, blue print hospital gown. The ushanka he rarely takes off, a fur-lined, Russian style hat with earflaps, is plopped on his head. A heap of stark white blankets lay over his body. He's a pitiful figure, but he's fine from what I can see. No one has harmed him.

Thank God.

"Hey," he says, his teeth chattering.

"Hey." I hug him, and he throws limp arms around my shoulders. When I kiss his cheek it's as cold as a corpse's.

"How you doing, bud?"

"Fine," he says, his clipped tone oddly formal. "How are you?"

"I'm okay," I say, but I don't want to stand there and exchange pleasantries.

"Sweetie, what were you doing out there with your clothes off?"

"I wanted to be free. Like the birds," he says. "God told me to follow the birds, and I did. They led me to this spot away from everything, and God told me to be free. So, I took off all my clothes."

"Kamau. . ." I begin, but I don't know what else to say.

"It's not wrong to be naked," he assures me. "Adam and Eve were naked."

He rambles on in his fractured reasoning about this. I try to convince him that he was on Lexmark's property and not in the Garden of Eden, but he's adamant that he's done nothing out of order. Finally, I give up and just listen. He prattles on, his teeth intermittently chattering.

I grab a chair and sit beside him, taking his hand. He's still so cold, and he sounds like he's out of his mind.

I've been waiting for an unmistakable sign. I finally have it.

12

Capgras Syndrome

Machines buzz and whirr around us while Kamau's hand warms in mine. His shaking ceases, and he drifts off to sleep. A tech dressed in green scrubs comes in and out, checking Kamau's vitals. His blood pressure is coming down.

Suddenly Kamau awakens. He yanks his covers off and glares at me. "You destroyed my family," he hisses.

My mouth opens, but words don't come out. I think he's blaming me for his father and me separating. Guilt rounds my shoulders. I did ask Ken to leave.

"Kamau, are you talking about me splitting up with your dad? I know it hasn't been easy."

"You know what I'm talking about."

A loud beep interrupts us. Kamau's IV fluids have run out. The same tech rushes in and replaces the bag. The annoying beeping stops, and the man leaves us alone again.

I return to the subject. "What do you mean I destroyed your family? If it isn't the separation, do you mean when I turned our living room into a painting studio? I did that for all of us," I say. "I wanted to change our lives, and I thought a new business would be just the thing. A creative business. I want you to paint there, too."

"I don't mean the studio. I like that. You know what I mean. You're acting like you don't."

I scoot my chair closer to him, and he recoils, so I lean back. "Baby, I'm really not sure how I destroyed our family. Will you tell me? I've always tried to take care of you."

He nods. "Mom always took care of us."

"I tried to make sure you had all that you needed, and then some."

"Mom was always the best, but you're not her. Get out of my face. I can't stand to look at you."

I'm shocked and hurt despite the fact that I know he's delusional. He's never, ever spoken an unkind word to me. I don't know how to react.

"I said get out," he bellows.

I stand up so fast, I nearly fall over the chair.

"Go, you, liar!"

I pull the chair to the other side of the curtain. When I speak my voice is reticent. "Kamau?"

"What?"

"I'll sit out here if I have to, but I won't leave you. I'm not going to leave you, do you hear? No one should be at a place like this alone."

I close the curtain and sit outside of his bed area. Another officer walks up to me, this one a burly White man of a higher rank than the cop who showed up at my door. He has papers in his hand.

"Sorry to do this to you, ma'am, but we have to press charges. What he did is a crime. But don't worry. They'll probably drop them. Just sign here."

Numbly, I take the pen he holds, place the papers on my lap, and sign my signature. I hand them back to him.

"Thanks," he says. He circles Kamau's court date and tears off a carbon copy for me. "Just show up on this day," he says, giving me the paper. "The case will probably get dropped."

The man walks away, and I sit there, outside the curtained area, feeling more alone than I have in a long time.

13

World's Worst Mother

A woman comes and talks to me about Kamau. She's the intake nurse. She's dressed in street clothes instead of scrubs. Her face is kind, but her performance of her duties brisk. She shoots questions at me like bullets.

When did the problems start? I saw a marked change in him last month.

How has he been sleeping? Poorly.

Is he on any medications? No.

What brought him into the hospital today? God told him to take his clothes off. Or birds. I'm not sure.

Is he in school? He's supposed to be taking online classes, but it's not going well.

Does he use any drugs? He smokes weed. I can't seem to get him to stop.

How do you get along? Fine when he knows I'm me, and not some imposter.

Is he violent? Never, but he wants to start an army.

Does he ever try to harm himself? Does he cut himself? Is he suicidal? No, no, no.

I tell her about January, when Kamau described his experiences on the bus and at the grocery store to me, and how his thoughts declined so quickly after that.

"I wasn't sure what to do.   I thought something had to happen more than weird ideas and terrible hygiene."

She nods, but I feel like I'm up for the world's worst mother award.

"I wasn't sure. I didn't know what to do."

She leaves me with my weighty guilt.

A psychiatric resident comes in and speaks with me. He asks the same questions, with a few new ones thrown in, then exits. I wait and wait, holding my waist and rocking in the folding chair outside of where Kamau lies sleeping. A movie of Kamau walking around naked, following birds, plays over and over in my mind. *I should have gotten him here sooner. Would they have even taken him? He seemed so normal, except for those thoughts.*

In all the years before or since my own diagnosis, I've never done anything as concerning as meandering about, naked as Eve, nor have I ever failed to recognize a beloved family member. It's clear to me now that he is sicker than I ever was, and I try not to think of what this could mean.

The intake nurse returns. The psychiatric team wants to admit Kamau. She'll give a report to the charge nurse upstairs and transport him to Behavioral Health. I nod, and the woman leaves me exiled in the folding chair, wishing I could say goodbye to my boy.

Kamau rests now, but my own thoughts fly like vultures circling memories until I'm back to 1996, in a psychiatric hospital after I'd attempted suicide. Screams and moans greet me as I step onto the unit, while slack-jawed, drooling Haldol zombies shuffle by. A middle-aged woman carrying a baby doll rubs the coarse blond hair on its plastic head and coos, "My baby." Would Kamau see these kinds of things when they take him upstairs? Would he be terrified, or terrifying?

14
Crazed: *1996*

The morning I was admitted to the hospital for a suicide attempt, I was a wild manic. Ken had come home at 6 a.m., after being out all night. Again. He was drunk, high off crack cocaine, or coming down from both. I attacked him as soon as walked into the door.

He tried to get away from me. He didn't want a physical altercation, but I was a Pit Bull Terrier, and Ken the chew toy in my locked jaws. I came on like a madwoman, unrelenting, leaving him little choice but to try and defend himself from my blows. When we were both exhausted from the altercation, I turned my rage on myself. I ran upstairs and took a bottle of Benadryl my doctor had given me to aid with my sleeplessness. There were seventeen pills left in the bottle. I had a fleeting thought that I didn't have to do it; I didn't have to take the pills, but there is something driving about bipolar compulsions. Mania lies. It makes you feel like you *must* spend the money, have sex with the person, take the pills, or jump off the building. I listened to the liar and swallowed all seventeen pink ovals.

Moments passed. I cried out to Ken, "I took some pills." But he would have nothing do with me. I had to be my own hero. I called 911.

When they arrived, I collapsed in an EMT's arms.

I wanted so much more for Kamau than this kind of drama.

15

The Best Thing: *1996*

At the hospital, wild-minded and broken, I found that I couldn't focus on anything. I wanted to read, but the words danced across the page. So, I ruffled the pages of a stranger's Bible back and forth like I was petting a strange bird. My hands flew across the thin edges of the paper until they stopped flat, and these are the words above all others that I saw.

"I am poor and needy, but the Lord hears me."

Tears stung my eyes, and I took a deep breath. That is the best thing I have ever heard about God.

Now, I close my eyes in silent prayer for my boy. I hope Kamau can somehow hear his own best thing.

16

The Kid's Unit

When it's time for us to go upstairs, the tech pulls the rails up on the gurney, raises the head, and allows Kamau to sit up while he wheels him onto the elevator. I trudge behind the pair at a distance I think will keep my child from going off on me again.

On the third floor, we pour out of the elevator to the left. Heavy double doors slam behind us. I feel like I've taken my son to a maximum-security prison.

As we pass the adult unit to get to the kid's side, I try not to look at anyone, and am grateful that there are no screams, drugged-out walking dead, or creepy ladies stroking their weird dolls. Past another set of double doors, the warmth of the adolescent unit, with happy murals of trees and birds native to Kentucky, welcomes us.

A fair-haired, soft-featured nurse with a no nonsense demeanor greets us. "I'm Wendy," she says, "and this must be Kamau."

I'm impressed that she says his name right the first time.

"I'm his mom, Claudia." Kamau doesn't disagree with me.

"I'll be your nurse," she says to Kamau, and he nods.

Wendy and the tech help him off the gurney, and I watch him check the place out. Kamau peers down the length of the short hallway. I ache to hold on to his hand, but feel more estranged from him than I've ever felt.

"We're going to go down to the Day Room," Wendy says. She points to the end of the hall. We follow her into a room about half the size of a classroom. Shelves stocked with board games, puzzles, books, and Legos line the walls. A TV with a Wii attached sits in the corner. I follow Wendy's lead and settle into a chair at one of several small tables crowded into the room, Kamau beside me in his hospital gown and silly Russian hat.

"This is where the kids have groups and spend their free time," Wendy explains.

She hands me a daunting stack of papers. "We'll go through them together."

Again, I have to answer questions about family history of mental illness. I tell her about my bipolar disorder, my dad's, and the aunt's. This whole business wearies me.

I want something else to blame, other than faulty DNA. It seems so unfair. Out of all my children, I'd have bet money that just about any of them would be here, other than Kamau. The more questions Wendy asks, the more upset I become. If the pitch of my voice rises any higher only dogs will be able to hear me. She asks about drugs.

"He smokes weed," I say, my histrionics peaking. "If he didn't smoke weed, this wouldn't have happened. Tell him," I demand. "Tell him how even weed can cause a psychotic break if you're predisposed to mental illness. Tell him he can't smoke weed at all."

Wendy is calm. She looks at Kamau and says, "Your mother is right." Then she looks at me. "But he's a teenager."

I do not want to hear this. Being a teenager means parties and concerts and basements hanging with his "boys," passing the joint. It's reefer madness, and in the end fate will find Kamau pushing a shopping cart full of God knows what, all around downtown Lexington. I think of what his life will be like after I'm dead, and an image of future Kamau assaults my thoughts. There he is, the unmedicated, mentally ill and stinky abandoned man, spitting on people and cussing them out for no reason, his hair matted, his clothing foul, and his shoes run down. My worst nightmare. He cannot. Ever. Smoke. Weed.

Wendy asks more questions, and I sign consent form after consent form. Finally, we're done. We follow Wendy through the unit. She shows us the dining space, and then Kamau's room. Ordinarily, I'd be able to visit with him for a bit, but she knows he thinks I'm an imposter. She tells us we should say goodbye, and I stretch my arms out to him, fairly desperate for a hug. Kamau walks into my arms, and hugs me back.

"Bye, Mom."

"I love you. I'll see you tomorrow. Be good." I kiss him on the cheek.

"I'm going to have to take the hat," Wendy says to Kamau. He surrenders it without a fight. Wendy hands me a folder with the parent's guide and the clothing the police had brought into the emergency room that Kamau had discarded at Lexmark. She tells me I can bring him in more clothing, as long as there are no strings or any inappropriate designs. "The parent guide will tell you more."

Someone escorts me out, and I take a last look at my boy, his tiny dreadlocks sticking up all over his head, the gown hanging on his shoulders. He doesn't look back at me.

When I get back home, I get in my car and drive right to Walmart. I know I can simply wash some of Kamau's clothes and take them to him, but I buy him three new outfits, a few extra T-shirts, socks, underwear, and house shoes. I try to choose things he will enjoy, shirts with comic book themes. Since we're Marvel people I buy an Avengers shirt. Later, at Barnes and Noble, as I pore over magazines he'll enjoy, I find a few tiny Marvel figurines to purchase. I also buy him a graphic comic Bible. It's too expensive, but I feel like I've failed him so profoundly that I overcompensate. When I drop these items off at the hospital, it feels like I've done penance.

When I arrive home, I wander into the studio like I've never been there before. I amble over to the little, black canvas sofa against the wall flanked by painting stations, and take his old clothing out of the clear hospital belongings bag. He'd left the house in his favorite jeans. I hold them up and smell them. They smell like a pair of several-days-worn, teenaged-boy jeans. I smile. So normal, and suddenly tears come.

My own manic wildness, aggression, sleeplessness, unseemliness, poor choices, and suicide attempts flood to mind at once. I know before any psychiatrist tells me that Kamau is bipolar, and the certainty that he can experience any of the horrible things I went through nearly fells me. I weep into the pants I still clutch, "My boy, my boy."

17

Visiting Day

It's Tuesday now, visiting day at the hospital, and I ask my boss if I can leave early to beat the traffic on Nicholasville Rd. Lumumba meets me at Good Sam. I've told him everything that happened, and he wants to talk to Kamau for himself. I don't think Mumba believes Kamau is really sick.

"He probably just wants attention, Mom," my firstborn tells me.

"I don't think so, Lumumba. It's pretty extreme to take off your clothes in February and go strolling around. I know the temperature has been mild, but not that mild."

"You don't know him like I do."

"Lumumba, this isn't attention seeking. I'm telling you, he's not doing well mentally. I'll bet he's bipolar."

"Maybe he's just still tripping."

Lumumba tells me that once when they were getting high, Kamau believed one of Mumba's neighbors was in danger, and kept knocking on the door, trying to save her.

"And as far as his thinking goes, Kamau is a visionary, Mom. He has this amazing mind. He's no joke."

"I know Kamau has an amazing mind, but Kamau is *losing* it. This is serious."

"I'll talk to him, Mom."

We wait outside the unit until it's exactly 5:30 p.m., when a Mental Health Associate ushers us back on to the kid's unit. Kamau's room is right by the nurse's station, strategically positioned because of the unpredictable nature of psychosis. He has no roommate. This means we can visit in his room.

When Kamau sees me, there's no doubt that he knows I'm his mother. He runs to me and throws his arms around my neck. I hold him for a long time.

I'm accustomed to seeing Kamau smile and laugh. I never see him cry, but this evening he's tearful, clinging to me like a frightened child.

"Mom, get me out of here. I don't want be here."

I squeeze him tighter. "I can't, sweetie. You're on a seventy-two-hour hold, otherwise, the police would have taken you to jail. We had to do it this way. It was either this or jail."

"But I didn't do anything wrong."

I lead him to the bed and sit him down, and settle myself beside him. "Kamau, I know you wanted to be free, but taking off your clothes in public is a crime."

"I just wanted to be like the birds and Adam."

"That's a beautiful thought, but this isn't a society you can do that kind of thing in, kid. You'll get in trouble for that, and you did, a lot of trouble. Kamau, one of your charges was resisting arrest. Do you realize the terrible things that could have happened to you if you had gotten the wrong police officer?"

He shakes his head, but I don't take him through the talk about how an unfortunate run-in with the law could have ended his life, and rendered his name a hashtag for justice-minded social media users. He looks so pitiful. I stick to the basics. "You can't walk around naked, Kamau."

His tears flow. "I won't do it again, I promise, Mom, I just want to go home."

"If I'd brought you here, I might be able to take you home, but I didn't bring you here. The police did. I can't take you out, bud."

He covers his face with his hands and his shoulders heave. I reach out and touch him. "I'm so sorry, bud."

Lumumba has watched this whole exchange. "Let me talk to him, Mom."

Almost everyone around me, I find out later, believes they can help Kamau snap out of this. Lumumba is convinced Kamau is faking, or if he isn't, he's just coming down from a bad trip. Still, they're brothers, and very close. I give them time alone to have this conversation I'll have no control over. I don't think a little talking can hurt, as long as they don't talk long.

While I'm waiting in the hall while Lumumba and Kamau huddle, speaking with voices too low for me to make out, the attending physician for the unit calls to speak with me. Her name is Dr. Kelly Hill. I take her phone call, standing just outside the nurse's station. My time with Kamau, with all his crying and begging me to get him out has already gotten me worked up. Once again, I tell our family's history, and everything that has happened as I knew it with the same increasing intensity bordering on hysterics I felt when I wanted Wendy to warn him about the dangers of weed. Dr. Hill is pleasant and patient. She tells me she wants to start him on Zyprexa, an antipsychotic medication that will help clear his thinking. I agree to this treatment. I'm not anti-medication. Not anymore. This is my child. If she suggests we do animal sacrifices to get him well, I'm saying yes like I was an Old Testament priest trying hard to appease a punishing God.

18

Adam

After my conversation with Dr. Hill, I plod down the hallway toward the Day Room. The Mental Health Associate, a striking, dark-haired man, who looks like a person more likely to sweep me up in a mosh pit at a rock concert, than care for my psychologically fragile son, greets me. His name is Adam. The irony of my Adam-the-first-man loving son having a caregiver named Adam does not escape me.

"I'm Claudia, Kamau's mom," I say. I don't extend my hand to shake and he doesn't offer his, but his smiling eyes assure me.

"It's good to meet you, Ms. Claudia."

Adam is seated at an open front metal school desk, a three ring binder resting on the oak laminate top. The desk is wedged in front of the door to the Day Room, and over his shoulder I notice a slumped shouldered girl inside, watching television. No visitors for her, I think, and this makes me sad. It also makes me feel guilty because I am not in my own child's room.

"I'm letting my sons have a little time alone," I say, hoping he isn't judging me for leaving my kid during the all too brief visiting hour.

He stands, and in a moment whisks a chair from out of the Day Room for me. He places it by the window beside his desk, and I notice the waning sun outside, the night soon to cloak the city.

Seated now, I look at Adam's kind face, and my mental health story explodes out of me in a chaos of words. I tell him about my faulty brain chemistry, its gifts, especially that of creativity, as well its propensity to lead me to take on what I would later realize are unfortunate choices. I share some of these poor choices in a rush of stories. Then I tell him how I hurt to see Kamau even more afflicted than I am. I'm not just afraid for my boy, I'm frantic. Not that he couldn't see that.

Adam listens to it all, making the appropriate empathetic noises, and even offering some of his own tangled history. He was a wildchild back in the day, and it appears to me that more than a little of that unfettered freedom remained in him. But he's safe now, I realize, and if he can be safe, can Kamau be? Can I?

A man of quiet faith, Adam encourages me to believe that good things are possible for my son. Good things.

Believe.

I tuck his words in the hushed space in my heart where I store all that is sacred to me, and when it's time to leave, I feel better than I had when I arrived.

19

Dr. Glaser

Zyprexa is an expensive drug. Medicaid, our health coverage, does not pay for it. However, on the phone, Dr. Hill mentioned that there is a way for Kamau to get the medicine. UK HealthCare's Child Psychiatry department has a research project going that explores the correlation between teens on Zyprexa and weight gain. The research project is only for adolescents with bipolar disorder or schizophrenia. Kamau qualifies. If he participates, the medication is free, but he would be required to go into the office once a week for nutrition counseling, and to have his weight checked and blood drawn. He is required to see the man running the study, Dr. Paul Glaser, before being accepted as a research subject.

I meet Dr. Glaser two days into Kamau's hospital stay. He is tall, and adorably nerdy, with a kind face and a demeanor that readily puts kids, and very nervous adults, at ease. He chatters with me about the study, and I can tell the hurting children he works with are important to him, but I'm half listening because I can sustain attention to almost nothing this week. I nod at what I hope are the appropriate moments and follow him into Kamau's room for his interview with my boy.

I take the chair at the desk near the foot of Kamau's bed. Dr. Glaser plops down on the edge of the mattress. He asks Kamau a series of questions whose answers I recognize could indicate bipolar disorder: has he ever felt so good that he did something that got him into trouble? That was an easy one. Has he felt so irritable that he lashed out at someone? Does he have racing thoughts or talk too much or too fast? They go on and on, Dr. Glaser's probing gentle, and Kamau's answers thoughtful. Yes, he has felt distracted. The television does talk to him. It tells him to go to war. Kamau is sure he is going to lose his left eye to the god Horus. He says these things matter-of-factly, and Dr. Glaser responds as if this is the most rational conversation he's ever engaged in. I am deeply impressed with this doctor who accepted Kamau's answers without a hint of alarm. I myself am visibly horrified that Kamau thinks the television is his Commander-in-Chief.

Dr. Glaser stands, thanks Kamau for his time, and asks if he may speak to me in the hallway. We leave Kamau in his room, and step into the quiet hall.

"I think Kamau would benefit from this study," he says. "He'll be able to get the medication he needs for free, and I'll talk with him at every session."

There was something about Dr. Glaser that I trusted. The way he listened. The way he saw my son. I wanted him to be Kamau's doctor. I wanted him to be my doctor. I wanted him to be everyone in the entire world's doctor.

"He thinks the television talks to him," I say, my voice tremulous.

"I think you're right about Kamau. I believe he is bipolar. What we would call textbook."

"It's . . ." I want to say it's crazy. He sounds like everything I know to be truly loco, but I abandon these terms. "It's so scary."

"We'll do everything we can to help him."

I believe him. I want my baby to be helped. A few minutes later, I'm sitting in the dining area signing more papers. When I'm done, Kamau is the newest participant in the Zyprexa study.

That's one thing done. What's next?

20

Reefer Madness

Two days after my talk with Dr. Glaser, I meet Lumumba in the parking lot of the Hospital, and together we traipse to the third floor to collect our loved one. I am worried and tense, sure that Lumumba will take Kamau on a monster marijuana smoke fest comparable to the famed Ann Arbor, Michigan Hash Bash. I am now convinced that weed is the devil, personified like the Jolly Green Giant.

"Don't smoke with him!" I screech at my oldest son. "It doesn't affect him like it does you, and it *could* affect you the same way, by the way." I prattle on about the dangers of wacky tobaccy like I'm an activist raising awareness of the connection between Mary Jane and psychosis. Lumumba ignores me all the way up to Behavioral Health.

As we walk through the adult unit and onto the kid's side, I remember my own harrowing hospitalization sixteen years earlier. No weed was involved in the making of that scary movie, but the harrowing fall out was just as insidious. That year I'd taken an overdose of pills after a violent altercation with my husband. Now, Kamau has paraded around naked. Both of us ended up losing our freedom for a time, and a good portion of our dignity. But I was okay. He would be okay, too, wouldn't he?

Kamau spotted us when we walked through the double doors, and bounded toward his brother and me with his big, gap-toothed smile. For a moment I felt as if I had my baby back. The grandiose maniac appeared to be gone, so was the suspicious, narrow-eyed stranger who had accused me of destroying his family. He enveloped me in the sweetest boy embrace, then gave his brother one of those awkward, manly pats-on-the-back side hugs. After more paperwork—there are always reams of paperwork in these matters—we walk out to the parking lot.

"I need a cigarette," my seventeen-year-old says.

"Don't start up again. You haven't had a cigarette for days. You don't need to go back to it." Next to drugs, cigarettes are the root of all evil these days. I want all his vices gone. I think this will protect him.

"Mom, I just want one."

"One is too many, and never enough." I have no idea where these slogans come from, but I'm a veritable motivational speaker against anything that will harm my child's delicate brain.

"Just one?"

I stone-faced deny him this request.

He and Lumumba climb into Mumba's truck, and leave me standing there feeling panicked and out of control. "Don't smoke. Anything!" I say one last time before they wave me away with promises of getting back soon.

Please don't smoke, I say to them in my mind, watching Lumumba's big, maroon Dodge peel out of the parking lot away from me. I know they can't hear me. Even if they could, they couldn't. Clutching the plastic patient bag of Kamau's belongings, I trudge to my Cavalier, already feeling defeated.

***

Of course, they smoke weed on their welcome home excursion. None of my pleading, nagging, or spouting statistics deter Kamau and Lumumba. They are brothers, and bandmates, best friends, and this is what they do, to celebrate, to commiserate, to grieve. To be fair, they didn't do much grieving, but if they did, smoking weed would be part of the ritual.

Lumumba clings to the wrong-headed notion that if he smokes *with* Kamau he can keep him safe. I cannot convince Lumumba that when one deals with bipolar disorder, very little is safe. I am not safe.

21

Family Christian

I return to work at Family Christian Stores. I'm a ridiculously inept employee, unfocused, but bright and funny. Customers like me. I'm Ms. Transparency, Saran Wrap in black pants and a white shirt. Disinhibited, I lack a proper filter. I talk too loud and too much about things inappropriate for the workplace. Kamau and I are descending into mental illness together. I'm terrified that I will either be flattened by depression, fly so high my hypomanic Icarus wings will fail, or both, simultaneously.

One Saturday afternoon, a regular visits the store. David's twinkling eyes and white beard conjure a kindly Santa. He works with homeless men and buys five-buck bibles by the box full. He asks how I am.

"I'm all right, but my son isn't. Will you pray for him?"

"What's wrong with your son?"

"He had a psychotic break." Because he smoked weed, I resist saying. "The doctors say he has bipolar disorder." I'm afraid to tell him about my own mental illness. A co-worker is near, and while apparently, I have no problem throwing Kamau under the stigma bus, I don't want them to think I'm unstable, even though I flew over the cuckoo's nest a long time ago, a behavioral health fact that's hard to miss about me.

David listens with a wry smile. He places the box of bibles on the counter for me to ring up. When I've told him about Kamau's confinement, he shares his own experience.

"They told me I was bipolar," he says, "but you know what that is?" He leans in, a bearded Santa slash Dr. Phil, with the Word of God and insider knowledge. "It's spiritual warfare. The devil is busy. Your son isn't bipolar. He needs deliverance."

I love working at the bookstore. It's sweet and squeaky, Jesusy clean. It has its challenges, however. I may not be a spiritual giant, but even I have trouble believing what is happening to Kamau is spiritual warfare, or it isn't in the way David is suggesting.

"Thank you!" I say beaming, as if instead of telling me my son has demon issues, he said I'm pretty with a girlish figure. I do not want to go there with him. I scan his bibles as fast as I can, and let him know how much I look forward to talking to him the next time he comes in.

But I can't let the idea go.

My sister Carly keeps coming to mind. We are so much alike, Carly and I, both of us women consumed by spiritual matters, only she is good and faithful, prophetic in her teaching during the Bible study for seniors we created, while I'm the one who does arts and crafts with the residents, or facilitates Bible Bingo when I can't get myself together enough to come up with a project to share. Carly is the John the Baptist of the two of us. I am an unnamed holy fool, or maybe just a plain old fool.

When I first tell her what is going on with Kamau, she is heartbroken. We speak of our beloved aunts, two struck with severe mental illnesses, and how even on their medication they are diminished. Yet, I'm certain that Carly believes as David does: what's happening to Kamau is spiritual warfare. The devil, who comes to kill, steal, and destroy, wants to claim my boy's life. I'm not so sure. I think there may be a modicum of truth to this, but at the same time, I believe what's happening to Kamau is rooted in brain chemistry. When I'm brave enough, I ask Dr. Glaser about this matter.

We are in his office. Kamau is in the waiting room. I broach the subject reticently.

"Dr. Glaser, I'm wondering if I could ask you something. Could Kamau be oppressed by the devil, or even possessed?"

His response is characteristically thoughtful. "We don't know very much about demons," he says. "But we do know a lot more about the brain since the time of Jesus. Sometimes the brain gets sick and needs medicine to feel better. This is something we know and have proof of."

I feel a little blessed assurance. There will be no exorcisms on my watch, but there will be much looking at Kamau's brain, trying to understand his thinking, and to sort out what is real, what is delusion, and what are the concerning gray areas in his gray matter.

That, and the goings on in my own brain, keeps me busy for another month.

22

April

Kamau was born on April Fool's Day. It fell on Good Friday that year. I should have known Jesus would owe me money for that boy. On Kamau's eighteenth birthday, as per usual now, I assumed my self-proclaimed role of his Protector-from-the-ills-of-Mary-Jane. He wants money to buy himself a present and a meal, a reasonable request.

I do not want to give him money. Money can buy dope. Kamau would think dope is an awesome birthday present, but Mama is not quite up for this kind of gesture. Guilt buffets me. My boy is turning eighteen. If I strapped myself to railroad tracks before a speeding train, I don't think I could convince him to give up smoking weed. No amount of pamphlets, statistics, anecdotes, testimonies of former users or current bipolar people convince Kamau that marijuana is his problem.

"It makes me feel better, Mom," he says, again and again. "It slows me down."

"Yes, it will slow you down because you'll end up in the hospital with a psychotic break."

I feel conflicted. I want him to have birthday money. I want him to get what he wants without my micro-management. Dr. Glaser once advised me not to give Kamau more than $10.00. I fold most of the time. I'm bad at being the mother of a mentally ill child.

Kamau ends up with a modest amount of cash, thirty-five dollars or so, and with that money I have purchased another burden of guilt.

23

Robert

As per Dr. Glaser's instructions, I immediately apply for Social Security Disability for Kamau. The tiniest part of me feels guilty, like I'm asking for a welfare handout, rather than trying to ensure my son will always have the means to receive medical care. There are more mountains of paperwork, more assessing appointments, and schlepping to the Social Security Administration office for yet another mound of papers to fill out.

Kamau is with me today. Even medicated he's vexed by unrelenting restlessness. He twitches and fidgets, paces and stalks a room like a young lion. He asks to go with me on errands, only to insist that he's bored and beg me to take him back home. And he chain-smokes cigarettes like the mentally ill person, with low impulse control, reeking of anxiety, that he is.

"Can I smoke in the car?" he asks.

"No." He knows I hate the smell of cigarette smoke. Denzel Washington wouldn't be allowed to smoke in my car, even if he trained his sexy bedroom eyes on me.

We ride in silence for a while, Kamau moving his long legs around in the passenger seat. He looks out the window. Taps a foot. Crosses his arms.

"Do you ever think about asking your godfather for help?" I ask him. Robert had been kind to Kamau in the past. He took him to the movies and out to eat. He even purchased him things Ken and I couldn't afford: a portable Play Station, a laptop computer for school work and gaming. He was a good man, though neither Kamau or I had much to do with him anymore.

Robert had welcomed me into the Eastern Orthodox Church. I believed that would be the last stop before heaven in my meandering spiritual journey. But it wasn't. Ultimately, the Orthodox Church seemed too strange, too difficult, and too austere. It also seemed too cultural, a culture that wasn't my own. I left in grief and became a Catholic. Robert was so angry that he began to call my friends to berate me and my decision to leave the Holy Orthodox Church. When that didn't work—they were *my* friends, after all—he began to talk down about me to Kamau. For all that he was, Kamau was a mama's boy who had never given me trouble until he grew ill. He wouldn't let anyone talk trash about his mama. According to Kamau, after one painful conversation too many, he vowed to have nothing else to do with Robert. I let it be his decision.

"Mom," Kamau says with a sigh, looking away from me as we whizz down Winchester Road, "Robert was a dirty old man."

I shoot a look at my boy. I had never heard him say anything like this about Robert. Robert was a Subdeacon at our former church. He chanted away on the altar, a heart rending and mending Divine Liturgy. He was a Black man, who by all appearances seemed to be the holiest soul in our parish. And he loved Kamau. For a time, he loved me like a sister.

"What do you mean, Kamau?"

"Mom, he had this video player set up in his car. He used to show me pornography all the time."

I have to focus so as not to wreck my car. "What?"

"He made me watch porn to give me all that stuff. It was like prostitution."

Terrible things have happened to me in my life. Some self-pitying days I believe I have had more than my fair share of suffering. I knew some truly awful people, one or two I would reluctantly label as evil, but not Robert. On several occasions I'd said to people, even after he excommunicated me from his life for becoming Catholic, that Robert was one of the best men I'd ever met.

I shook my head. The fact that Robert, Kamau's Godfather, a man I entrusted to teach my son about the Church, would use his time with my boy to expose him to pornography devastated me. We met Robert when Kamau was eleven.

Eleven.

I take a deep breath, keep my eyes on the road ahead, and ask the question that I have to, a nightmare of a question that I cannot *not* ask.

"Did he ever touch you?"

Kamau pauses. I don't look at him. I don't want to embarrass him.

"Once," he said, the biggest little word I've ever heard.

"I am so sorry, Kamau. I am so so very sorry."

He assures me—sweet boy—that it isn't my fault. I think I will never believe it.

"Don't tell anyone, Mom. I don't want anyone to know."

"But…"

"Please, Mom. This is just between you and me."

"Okay," I nod. I won't tell anyone."

We ride the rest of the way in silence, Kamau watching the scenery roll by, and me trying hard not to wail.

***

Home again, I do not keep my word. The first thing I do is tell my daughter, Abbie, what Robert had done.

"What?" she says, her expression as stunned as mine must have been when I heard the news. But she doesn't seem to wonder how this could be. She accepts it immediately and prepares to retaliate.

"I'm going to kill him."

"What am I supposed to do?"

I ask this person who is my child for advice. Even though she is an adult now, she's really not the person with the answer.

"I'm going to kill him," she says, her tone more resolute than before.

"And I'm supposed to let him get away with it?" My shock and sadness has given way to anger. I want him to pay. I don't want to betray Kamau's trust, although I just did, but I need to process what I heard. I need to make a decision, one that may not be the one Kamau wants. "He shouldn't get away with it, looking all holy."

"I should have known," Abbie says. "I always thought he was gay."

"I thought he was gay, too, but I didn't think he was a child molester."

Abbie and I rant until I go to my room for the night. I'm still not finished processing. I sit down on my bed and call Kamau's dad to tell him the sordid news.

A pause. A heavy sigh. I hear the same devastation in his voice that is in my own when he says, "I am going to destroy that man."

"Me, too," I say. "Kamau doesn't want me to tell anyone. He doesn't want police involved."

Ken doesn't respond to this. After his stony silence, blame pours out of him. It's all my fault. He knew there was something about that man. I take that blame because I should have seen this coming. I should have prevented it. Robert wasn't generous. He wasn't extraordinarily kind. He was a predator who groomed my son to be his victim.

Ken and I don't talk for long. I hang up the phone and climb under the covers, clothes still on, more exhausted than I've ever been. Kamau is out on one of his walks again. I try my best not to blow an aneurysm from worry.

Sometimes

***

It seems like everything is going in fast motion, and I am a sloth with a limp. I can't keep up with appointments. With medication. With homeschooling. Everyone is on their own, whizzing ahead of me, and I'm running to catch up, but they're too far gone, while I'm going in slow motion, failing at everything.

24

April 27, 2012

Kamau sits at the desk we've propped against the narrow wall between the kitchen and the studio, trying hard to focus on his online high school completion work. PLATO, a home-schooling program Fayette County uses for troubled students who can't be in a classroom, has been a bust for him.

Even medicated, his manic states have made it impossible for him to concentrate on the work. Today his efforts are futile. The birds, he tells me, have been trying to get him to follow them.

"The birds?" I fail to hide the wariness in my voice. "Kamau, are the birds talking to you again?"

"They always do."

"What do they say?"

He shrugs a wide shoulder. "They tell me I need to be like them. I need to be free."

Panic washes over me in waves as he chatters on about the birds and their instructions. I don't want to listen. I don't want to hear this kind of talk, but it's the only way I can gauge how sick he is, and he is very sick. Seemingly all of a sudden.

We had been doing so well. He'd taken his meds from me without incident, and I felt confident that I could entrust him to continue on his own with few reminders. Each morning and before bedtime, I asked, "Did you take your medicine, Kamau?" He would answer my queries with unequivocal yeses. So why was he in communion with the fowl of the air again?

"Kamau," I repeat, as even-toned as I can, "have you been taking your medicine?"

Despite his previous assertion that he has, he answers honestly now. "Not really. Mom, I don't want to take that stuff. It makes me feel weird."

"Weird how?"

Another broad-shouldered shrug. "I don't know. I just don't feel right."

"How long have you been off your medicine?"

"A few days." Even a few un-medicated days are too many. I march into his room and take the bottle of Zyprexa off his chest of drawers, then storm down the hall again, screwing the cap off the bottle, stopping only long enough to pour him a glass of water from the tap.

"Take it," I say, thrusting the glass at him,

"Mom. . ."

"Do you want to end up in the hospital again? Take it."

Kamau sighs and begrudgingly pops the pill into his mouth, followed by a few gulps of the water.

"Let me see."

He opens wide and allows me to peer into his mouth. When I'm satisfied he hasn't cheeked the pills, I look into his eyes. "Don't ever do that again." But authoritarian parenting has never been my style. Already I'm afraid Kamau is going to find a way to get out of consuming the one thing I feel sure is standing between him and insanity.

Kamau sighs and gestures toward the computer. "Mom, I can't do PLATO. I just want to get a GED." This, I anticipated. We'd tried this online school option, tried hard, but his mind is a jungle and the jumble in his head makes any sustained focus impossible.

"I'll drive you to the Fayette County Public School's office to withdraw, and we'll get you signed up to take GED classes."

I'm not sure if this will work either, but once again I'm at a loss as to what to do.

In a little more than a month, Kamau will be eighteen, and he'll have to learn to make his own, hopefully good decisions. I'll have to give him room, fall or fly.

After I'd taken him to the office, only to have him decide to try PLATO again, I take a long look at him before he gets into the car. He is beautiful. His hair, recently cut and dreadlocks free, is already growing back, and he's twisted the dark curls into what will become a new set of locks. When he smiles at me, a strange, sad, lost little boy smile, I feel of rush of protective instinct slash through me.

I silently wish him happiness. I wish him freedom, few of the tragedies, and all of the triumphs those of us gifted with bipolar brains are given. *May you soar*, I think, before he climbs into the back seat.

When we arrive home, he tells me he wants to take a walk to his brother's apartment.

"Don't stay out late," I tell him. "I want you to take your night meds on time."

"Okay," he says, "I love you, Mom."

"I love you, too." The sorrow in his brown eyes moves me, but I don't know how to fix it. It will get better, I tell myself, but I don't believe it. Not one little bit. I'm waiting on the next big thing, the second unmistakable sign that will tell me he needs to go to the hospital, because it's coming. What I don't know is just how soon.

25

From WKYT Online: *9:10 PM*

*P*olice are investigating after a man fell from a downtown Lexington parking garage on Friday night.

Witnesses tell WKYT they saw the man fall from the upper level of the garage at Broadway and Short Streets. They tell us he grabbed a wire connected to a light pole before hitting the pavement face down. They believe he was very young, possibly in his late-teens or twenties.

"We saw him face down, half on, half off the curb. You could tell his teeth had been fractured. They were messed up, and blood was just everywhere on his face," said a witness.

Police blocked off part of Broadway between Main and Short Streets to investigate. They are not sure if the fall was an accident or deliberate.

26

Short and Broadway

A doctor and three trauma nurses are eating at deSha's Restaurant in Victorian Square. The building is catty-cornered from the parking structure. Their meal is disrupted when they notice people gather at the window, looking at some spectacle outside. They're watching my boy laid out on the ground. When they see what is happening, they rush outside and become his first responders. They gently move his head back and clear his airway so that he doesn't die before he reaches the hospital. A man in a suit, a passerby, holds Kamau's hand. He tells him over and over, "Everything will be all right."

Later, I meet one of the nurses. She says, "On the way to him, all I could say was Jesus, Jesus, Jesus." I cry as I hug her.

Part Two

27

Charlie Brown: *Day 1*

The night I screech at nurse Charlie Brown—*good grief*—about how I have to go home and rest or I'll get sick, I don't sleep much. In those few hours of restless quiet, away from the horror of my son's broken body, my mind pieces together a narrative. It's a crazy quilt of facts and feelings that tells a story. In the beginning I had a beautiful boy. In the middle he lost his mind. And now, at the end—is this the end?—Kamau took to the air on his own wings, and the wind did not hold him. So much ended here, both of our lives as we knew it. I have no idea what our new life will bring.

My job ends, too. I call into Family Christian Stores breathless with shock the April morning after Kamau's fall.

"My son fell off of a building."

There is a sharp intake of breath on the other line. Then understanding, "Go take care of your boy." I will never go back to that job though I don't know it at the time. I only know for now I'm going to need to be at the hospital as much as possible, for my sake as much as Kamau's.

As Charlie Brown ushers me to Kamau's bedside, she chatters on about how it's a miracle that he didn't break his neck falling face first. It gives her chills. She holds her arms out and shows me the goosebumps rising on her flesh. I'm silent, trying to steel myself to see him. And there he is.

The crowd of professionals working on Kamau is gone. He is alone on a bed. Propofol keeps him unconscious, and this is a great mercy. Tubes snake in and out of his brown body. His flat face spills over the cervical collar bracing his neck, and he looks like a fun house version of my son, distorted by a trick mirror. I want to shove my fist in my mouth to keep from screaming, but I stay mute until the back of my throats hurts from the effort.

"He's a little miracle," Charlie Brown chirps again, leaving me with Kamau, and I nod, thinking of miracles, and how they often happen when something terrible has taken place. When Jesus raised Lazarus from the dead, it was a miracle, but Lazarus still had to be dead a few days to qualify. Jesus still wept when he heard his friend was dead. Miracles don't necessarily come without you getting your ass handed to you first.

I pull up a small uncomfortable chair and sit beside him. In my mind Kamau falls a thousand times. I think about the pain he must be in when he's awake. How does one tolerate a body so broken, a face that is shattered? Tears track down my face.

My poor baby.

A toppling wave of grief washes over me, nearly pulling me under. I want to be strong for my boy, but now I'm not. All I can think of is my baby hitting that ground, over and over again. "I can't bear it," I cry, "I can't."

I fumble to get my phone out of my purse, and dial my friend Lisa, the first person who comes to mind. When she answers, I choke out the words on repeat in my head. "I can't bear it."

"Claudia, I can't understand what you're saying."

My words tumble over each other in my anguish, but I can't stop weeping.

"Are you at the hospital?"

Somehow, she is able to make out my yes.

"I'm on my way," she says, her voice unfaltering. "Just hold on."

I hang up the phone, and rock, holding on to my waist. A song comes to mind, one I used to sing to the kids when they were babies. This time I have to mother myself. I choke out the words while I rock myself calm: *Jesus loves me this I know. For the Bible tells me so. Little ones to him belong. They are weak, but he is strong…"*

Lisa finds me like that, singing and rocking, and places her hand on my shoulder. I stand and fall into her embrace.

I've believed for a long time in incarnational Christianity. God works through people. I need Jesus' gentle love in that moment, and it comes through her strong arms. She is mercy made manifest, and I am strengthened by her compassion.

Later, I am calm. Lisa sits in a chair next to mine beside Kamau's bed, and we speak quietly.

"What are the doctors saying?"

"They don't know the extent of his brain injury. As of last night, all they can say is that he can give a thumbs up in response to questions."

We are silent again, the weight of the doctor's misgivings press down on my heart. I feel breathless with anxiety. "Pray for him."

"I will," Lisa responds, such tenderness in her voice. "I knew I loved Kamau before this, but I didn't know how *much* I love Kamau until now."

I know exactly what she means.

28

Luf: *Week 1*

Word of Kamau's accident spreads fast, but because I'm so distressed I don't realize that what happened has been on the local TV news, as well as reported in the newspaper, the *Lexington Herald Leader*, both print and online editions. I only know more people are reaching out. They bring me envelopes full of cash and deliver prepared meals to my home. Their solicitousness moves me.

By now I can reach out, too. I send small dispatches on Facebook. I ask for prayers, and report on how Kamau is doing. Hundreds of people respond. Lisa uses pictures on Facebook of Kamau from the time he was a preschooler to his senior year in high school and makes a collage. I fall in love all over again with that face, at three-years-old, and seven, and seventeen.

Ken's friends show him kindness as well. One loans him money to make the trip to Kentucky, and he joins me. On the night he arrives, we make the trip to University of Kentucky Chandler Hospital, even after his long drive. I try to prepare Ken for what he will see, but he says, "I'm all right," and walks in the room without hesitation. He goes to his unconscious boy and places his hand in his and stands there with him. I don't know what he's thinking, but I say a prayer for them. How ever fractured our family is, whatever bad blood there is between us, I am glad Ken is here, and that Kamau has his mom and his dad.

The doctors wake Kamau intermittently. This is to gauge his progress and responsiveness. They wake him while we are present.

"Kamau," the resident says loudly, as if the man thinks Kamau has lost his hearing in the fall. And then he proceeds, asking him a series of questions which require a thumbs up answer. I do not remember these questions, but they must have been remarkably affirmative to always require a thumbs up answer.

Kamau winces in pain, and I catch a glance at his broken teeth. God, I can hardly stand the idea of him suffering. I want him to get back to the bliss of drug-induced sleep as soon as possible. Cotton pads that resemble tampons are stuck in Kamau's nostrils, as a foul-smelling drainage pours from his face constantly. I cannot image the agony of a broken face. I can't even tolerate a toothache.

Finally, the resident is done. The nurse is medicating Kamau again. He will be under soon, so Ken and I say goodbye.

"I love you, Mau," Ken says.

"Love you, bud," I say.

Using what has to be much of his strength, Kamau mouths one syllable that sounds like "luf."

29

Rebel

One early afternoon, Kamau's friend Michael contacts me on Facebook Messenger and asks if he can visit. Of course he can, I say, and I try my best to prepare him for what he will see as gently as I can. He arrives one afternoon, a brooding, brown-haired, coltish boy, bearing a collage he's made full of images of rebellion. I walk him into the room, slowly. He takes the steps to Kamau's bed on his own while I retreat to the corner of the room, my eyes on him.

They are comrades, Michael and Kamau. I knew my son got weed from Michael. Neither of them know that I'm aware of this. They are anarchists, rock 'n' roll rebels. It is them and their boys against the whole damned world. Michael stands in front of Kamau for a few moments. He doesn't say a word. If he has questions, if he has whys, he doesn't articulate them.

Michael sniffles, and his shoulders shake. He is trying to be strong, but he is not. The tears fall despite himself. Michael cries as quietly as possible, although I am being very unobtrusive. I don't let him see that his tears have made me cry as well. I quickly wipe my eyes, and walk out of the room, giving him time.

I leave the collage propped against the wall.

A memory of myself, just a little older than Kamau, losing my mind flies into my thoughts. Back then I pored over the suicide poets, Sylvia Plath and Anne Sexton. I was desperate to find anyone who felt as deeply as I did, feelings that soared heavenward and dipped into hell, a blessing and curse to experience. I marvel that I survived those days, and think about my boy and his terrible fall. Was he following the birds? Or did he grow weary of feeling all the feels and try to end it all? Both scenarios are feasible.

I go back into the room. Michael touches Kamau's hands and promises to return. I thank him for coming, then sit by my boy again. Later, teams of doctors come to tell me once again that things are hopeful.

30

Kid Brother

When some of the swelling has gone down, doctors want to do the first of possibly several surgeries to repair Kamau's face. They will use plates and screws, and in some cases, build where the bone has shattered in pieces so tiny they cannot be pieced back together. I do not understand how they will transform a jigsaw puzzle to my handsome boy again, but a sweet, earnest surgeon tells me he will take a copy of the collage of Kamau photos that Lisa has created to use as models in the operating room. He tells me, "I'm going to operate on him like he's my kid brother."

31

Why Me?

One day my sister Carly and I are driving down the street. We are talking about my bipolar disorder, how Kamau inherited it, and how now this awful thing that has happened to him. She asks a startling question.

"Do you ever wonder why you?"

I think I know what she is getting at. I may be wrong, but I believe she is wondering if my sins have caused this evil to visit my house. Or my unbelief. I have not been a model Christian. I am not the picture of faithfulness to God.

I shake my head. "No. I don't."

I never wonder why me. If I know anything, it's that the rain falls on the just and the unjust. I've learned from praying "God, this is some bullshit" enough times that be I good or bad, sometimes terrible things happen, but God, be I good or bad, is with me in the suffering. I don't know why Robert molested Kamau. I don't know why my Kamau went psychotic. I don't know why he jumped off a building, or for that matter, why I'm prone to losing my own my mind. I only know that when I find myself like the Biblical demoniac, spiritually naked, mentally chained, and howling out of my head, it is Jesus that shows up breaking chains and releasing me. If he doesn't, he at least stays until I'm calm again. No matter what, it is he who quiets my screams and steadies my thrashing.

32

Ex-girlfriend

By now I have heard from several people, but not Kamau's ex-girlfriend. I don't know if she's been told about the accident, but she was his first love. She was with him when the psychosis began. His descent into madness had to be hard for her. I know she cared deeply for Kamau, and I want her to know how badly he is hurting, how much he needs any modicum of support I can rally from anyone who ever loved him.

She is Kamau's friend on Facebook. I send her a message, explaining it all, his early signs of mania, the psychosis, the crazy talk that surely confused her, the fall. I don't hear back from her, not even a perfunctory "I'm sorry. Kamau will be in my thoughts."

Not long after, I get word from her mother saying that any messages to her daughter needs to come through her. It turns out her mother survived the suicide of a boyfriend when she was a senior, and she wants to protect her daughter from the pain and suffering she endured.

I understand this. The mother in me empathizes with the mother in her, but I am, above all, Kamau's mom, and he is not dead. I am greedy for any boost to his morale I can dredge up. At this point and forevermore it's unclear whether Kamau tried to commit suicide. Yes, she needs to protect her child, but I need to protect mine by surrounding him with the love of his friends, including his first love, even though their relationship has ended. The whole situation paints another layer of sorrow across my grief.

Later, the one mutual friend of ours gives me a fist full of money. She says, "It's from a friend who wants to remain anonymous." I'm almost certain it's from his ex's family and accept the money with gratitude, but it feels like some kind of atonement, no matter how I try to talk myself out of the idea.

33

Sometimes

I lie in bed at night, and a flock of wild anxieties soar in circles around my aching head.

34

Haircut

On the day of Kamau's first surgery, a nurse shaves part of his head. She goes for necessary hair removal, not pleasing appearance. Weird afro tufts stick out willy-nilly from the back of his head. When he is awake, I lean over and say, "Kamau, you have the worst haircut ever."

He smiles at me.

35

The 23rd Psalm

It is the morning of Kamau's first surgery. Without the aid of Propofol, he writhes in agony in bed until he finally settles and sleep overtakes him. I hold his hand and pray the 23rd psalm over him, repeating this line several times: "Surely goodness and mercy will follow you all the days of your life."

"You are strong, Kamau," I say to my boy.

He squeezes my hand.

36

St. Michael

Fearful of what will happen in surgery today, I pray. "St. Michael the Archangel, defend us in battle. Be our protection against the wickedness and snares of the devil. May God rebuke him, we humbly pray, and do Thou, O Prince of the Heavenly Host, by the Divine Power of God, cast into hell Satan, and all the evil spirits that roam the earth seeking the ruin of souls."

That same day I get a message from a mystically inclined friend in an online artist's group I'm a part of. She says, "A rather large archangel has not moved from Kamau's side since the accident."

This feels like a miracle, and since I've already had so many, I believe her.

37

New Face

The first surgery is to repair Kamau's upper and lower jaw, and rebuild his nose and cheekbones. It's a long, grueling surgery, scheduled from 7:30 a.m. to 6:10 p.m. After they  take him back, I wait nervously in the surgical waiting room, my iPhone close by. I shoot messages to my Facebook followers, updating them on his progress, and friends all over the world pray hour by hour for him and wait with me. I think of Kamau's face that I knew so well and loved so much, and am unspeakably sad. How will I say goodbye to his beautiful face for good?

No one tells me I will grieve the loss of Kamau's good looks. His lovely gap-toothed smile has crumbled. The front of his skull is in pieces. Now doctors are trying to put it together again like they are Humpty Dumpty's king's horses and men. The awful truth is I will miss the son I had. The way *he* looked. And I have yet to fall in love with the boy they'll wheel out of the operating room, the kid whose face will be held together by plates and screws and, for all I know, Dr. Frankenstein like creations I don't understand.

Hours pass. The operating room sends text messages informing me that the surgery is going well. I update my Facebook friends, and wait, praying, and trying hard not to be an asshole about how Kamau is going to look when this is all over.

When they wheel him out, Kamau's face is swollen, and one

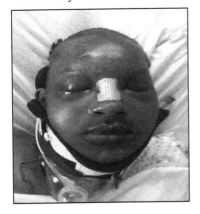

cheek is noticeably larger than the other, but he looks good, and I push back any feelings of loss in favor of deep gratitude for a surgeon that took a boy with a broken face, and treated him like he was his kid brother. Kamau is beautiful in the way he is beautiful now, not before. For what it's worth, I'll take it.

38

Sometimes

No matter how hard I try, sleep eludes me.

39

After

Three days after his surgery, Kamau's violent thrashing lands him in four-point restraints. But he tries, several times, to sit up so Ken and I can hold him.

40

Ten Days Later

K amau sits up in a chair for the first time. He even stands
with help, briefly.

41

Patient Safety Companion

Kamau is awake more often now, but he is a sick, sick boy. He spends hours trying to pull out his trach tube and curling into himself and rocking like a roly-poly bug with all his might, that is when he is not trying to get out of bed. A wondrous being called a Patient Safety Companion or "sitter" has been added to Kamau's caregivers. This person's sole responsibility is to keep Kamau safe when he is otherwise unattended. I marvel at these beings. They provide round-the-clock service, gently alerting a nurse when Kamau is trying to get out of bed, or pull on his tubing, or do anything unsafe.

They are here as he sleeps, and I'm grateful. They are the angels in the room. I cannot be at the hospital twenty-four hours a day. Ken stays for two weeks, but can't afford to be away from his job any longer. I live right next door to a nightclub. Sometimes the revelers get rowdy after hours. My girls don't like to be left alone, so I sleep at home. I trust that the sitter will watch over my child in my absence.

I know they will not love him like I do. But some sitters grow deeply attached to him, as well as to Aziza and me. One sitter is Kirsten, an older women and expat from Denmark. She's what one would call a talker and foodie who regales us with endless tales about her culinary adventures. I relieve her from the boredom of sitting with Kamau and she relieves us of the monotony of hospital life by taking Aziza for ice cream or grilled cheese sandwiches in the hospital cafeteria.

I ask Kirsten about sitting. It's been three weeks, and, though it's unimaginable, I'm going to have to get back to work. Because I simply never returned, and at some point, failed to continue to call in, I don't even consider returning to Family

Christian Stores. I smell the smoke from the bridge I burned. According to Kirsten, sitting is an easy gig, and the work is readily available. She tells me the name of the person I need to contact, and I file it away for future reference.

42

Today

I am hunched over Kamau, worry etching my face. How will we ever get past this? Then, as if he can read my thoughts, Kamau, slowly, painstakingly, stretches out his hand, finds my head, and stokes my curls, as if to comfort me.

43

Progressive Care

Twelve days after his accident, Kamau steps down from the Intensive Care Unit, to Progressive Care. Ken writes on my Facebook page. "Wondering if progressive care is for the parents or for those responsible for a patient. After some time, you don't even call the nurse. You just do things without much thought because you know they need to be done. You also do other things, like have a conversation, hold a hand, or say I love you. I've progressed a great deal, and I care even more." I'm grateful for his help, and that he's here.

44

The Second Surgery

Kamau's eyes were significantly damaged in the accident. Doctors murmur concerns about his brain injury and the possibility of him going blind because his eyes aren't doing well. I am afraid for this surgery to go on. Everything feels precarious today.

Success

Kamau's eye socket is so badly damaged it cannot be repaired; it has to be rebuilt. I don't care if the doctors do this with spit, duct tape, and fractured prayers; I'm just happy it's done. They rebuild his eye sockets with a complex material they explained to me, which I promptly forgot. My child can still see, and he looks good. That's enough for me.

45

Job Coach

My life may have lurched to a halt, but my bills didn't, and the kind one hundred-dollar gifts and twenties pressed into my palms have stopped coming. People move on, and we are left to deal with our stuff on our own.

I need to pay a water bill and have scant resources left. I know Catholic Charities is one of the few organizations that help and humbly seek their assistance. They require you to see a job coach if you're unemployed. I qualify.

I meet Jim at Community Ventures, a small business support organization. He's a tall, thin man, salt and pepper-haired. He's wearing khakis and a brown plaid shirt. Short of lumberjack, I can't imagine what he does for a living. He doesn't say.

Jim shakes my hand with a firm pump, then we sit. As is common for me now, I blurt out the story of Kamau's accident with accompanying histrionics.

I wish I were poised. When my nephew Justin was murdered, his mother Joy was a lesson in grace. She calmly, tearlessly greeted every mourner at his funeral. She smiled and hugged us. She comforted us. But I seem to live, howling, in sackcloth and ashes, with a takeout box of ashes in hand for later. Kamau isn't even dead, but his story, and the grief that accompanies it, clings to me like ashes of the dead flung in a damp wind, sticking to my face.

Jim listens intently and waits patiently for me to settle down. Finally, he speaks.

"It's going to be very difficult for you to work. Your son is in the hospital, very sick, and from there, he's probably going to go to some kind of rehab facility. There will be doctors' appointments to keep. You're going to need a job that's very flexible."

"Yeah," I quip. "Nice work if you can get it, and I can't get it."

46

God's Secret Weapon

To take away some of my burden, my sister Carly moves in with the girls and me. We go to Walmart that first day and laugh and laugh at floral house-dresses we swear we are going to buy.

"We'll be two old Black women in house dresses. Nobody will suspect us of anything," I say.

"We'll be God's secret weapons. Praying and fasting, and tearing the devil's kingdom down," Carly decrees.

"We're going to plant flowers and have a garden. It's going to be great."

We buy impatiens because they explode into color as they grow. I buy mini-cucumbers and tomatoes we name Sugary at the farmer's market. We never get the house dresses, and I don't do much fasting, but I'm always praying, usually, "Please help."

Carly's prayers seem more effective. She keeps us going.

47

Talking

Kamau has his trach tube replaced with a smaller one that will allow him to talk. After weeks of silence, the change is welcome. I'm sure he has questions. I have questions, too. I don't know what, if anything, he remembers.

He doesn't talk right away, but I'm used to the quiet. One night, late, I'm with him. It is near the end of a *Law and Order: Special Victims Unit* marathon, and I'm watching Elliott and Olivia's latest bust when Kamau speaks, startling me so much that I jump up from the chair.

"Mom, can you help me with this?" are his first words in over a month.

"Whoa!" is my response, because I haven't heard a peep except when he mouthed, "luf" that one time. He had gotten his tubing a bit tangled, and I snapped to it to fix the problem.

Kamau's eyes search mine. "What *happened*?"

"You fell from the top of a parking structure. The one at Short and Broadway. Do you remember falling?"

He shook his head. "When?"

I think this amnesia is a mercy. Then he breaks my heart anew.

"What about Robert?"

What. About. Robert? I'm stunned that this is what he says when he can finally speak again.

Kamau has been in the hospital for weeks now. He can't walk. According to doctors, he has at least a year of recovery ahead of him. I had to choose one struggle, and my injured boy was it.

"I don't know, Kamau, but I'll figure it out. I promise. Let's get you better first."

He didn't talk anymore that night, and I turned off SVU, wondering if that made him think of Robert in the first place. But I tucked his question deep within, in a place I put the concerns I care most deeply about.

48

Vision

It is early afternoon. The sun warms us beyond the hospital window, but it brings no pleasure. I am in tears, sitting in the bed with Kamau. He is, too.

He is my bud, my little flower, bound as tight as a fist. He arrived early in the world, five weeks, a wee, four-pound warrior, a baby who would not cry when nurses poked him with a needle. Now here he is as vulnerable as he was when he was a preemie, and just as tough, because against all odds, he's alive.

His shattered face has been rebuilt. Doctors have wired his jaw shut for healing, and with their gentle ministrations, tended to his traumatized brain. He slept for almost two weeks, but today he's awake and grappling with whys. He doesn't remember what drove him to jump off that parking structure. He only knows he woke up in a hospital, his former life gone, his future uncertain. He cries a lot today. We both do.

"I had a vision, Kamau," I tell him while tears spill from my own red-rimmed eyes. "It wasn't anything supernatural. Just a look into the future with faith, hope, and love." What I don't tell him is how miracles almost always take place when something terrible has happened. In the midst of catastrophe, you say yes. Yes, to Jesus' question, "Will you be made whole?" Yes, to a life beyond what you thought was possible in your pain. You somehow say your yes with everything in you. You believe in its possibilities.

"I see you one hundred percent better," I say, "You are whole, and not only that you are inspirational."

He cries harder and chokes out the words, "I hope so."

Hope is good. Even when it comes holding the hand of uncertainty.

"I hope so," he says again, as if repeating it will make it so.

I don't mention how afraid I am for him some days, or how the loss of the face I once adored leaves a raw ache in me. I don't say how much I miss his gap-toothed smile. I simply bend over and press my lips onto his new face built of ruins. I sing to him of his beauty right now: *You are beautiful in every single way,* and I stifle the unrelenting scream lodged just at the back of my throat.

Hope, a resilient little four-letter word. The need for hope suggests hopelessness. But sometimes you have to craft a vision while the nightmare still troubles your awakening.

"Don't you cry, son," I tell my boy again through a veil of tears. "I see you one hundred percent, and more than that, you are an inspiration."

"I hope so," he says.

I hope, too, enough for both of us. Maybe even all of us.

49

Sometimes

The best part of my day is when I see Kamau. The hospital is an escape from all. That. LIFE. It's quiet. Kamau doesn't watch television. He is as sweet as a toddler, tender and kind, and every now and then I climb in his bed to hold him. Sometimes, being with him takes the edge off the harshness of the world, and I can breathe a bit.

50

Nia

Aziza and I make a daily trek to see Kamau, most of the time twice a day, in the mornings and at night. Abbie and Lumumba have been to see him several times, but Nia hasn't been at all. Kamau has been in the hospital weeks by now, and today my guilting works. She agrees to go.

Nia, ZZ, and I arrive just as the nurse and techs are trying to stand Kamau up. He is weak, and his legs wobble beneath him. Kamau has spent much of his time in the hospital unconscious and intubated. The amount of weight he's lost is striking. Now, here is Nia, walking into the room seeing this thin, frail, kid with a face that isn't quite the same as her brother's. She is silent, a self-conscious fourteen-year-old girl. She slinks away to the side of the room.

"Hey, Mom! Hey, ZZ, Nia," Kamau says, interrupting the work of standing. ZZ and I speak, but Nia remains mute. The nurse and techs sit Kamau in a chair. He won't stand up on his own today, but they had to try. The staff excuses itself, and I exchange a few pleasantries with my boy, then look at Nia. Tears are streaming down her face. She is devastated by what I've had weeks to process. I am watching her heart breaking.

"Can we go, Mom?" she says.

I know she needs this time. I kiss my boy on the forehead, gather my girls, and we leave the hospital as fast as my car can carry us away. She doesn't talk on the way home, and I don't fill the space with senseless chatter.

Sometimes

***

I find myself talking to strangers, telling them what happened to Kamau. I talk too loud and too fast. I want to laugh for some reason. I want to cry, and I want to holler all at once. I feel the ragged, threadbare thing holding me together beginning to unravel. I pull at the threads, sometimes right in front of the stranger, and watch as something terrifying falls out of my mouth.

51

What Happened

Another night alone with Kamau, and I am trying to wait it out past eleven o'clock when the parking attendant leaves so I will not have to pay for parking. Hospital life is expensive, and every little hack I can find I utilize. I am watching *Law and Order: Special Victims Unit* again. It does not occur to me, because we've watched this show at our house like it is the only show on the air for years, that it could be triggering to Kamau.

He looks at the screen. Points at the child victim. "That's what happened to me. What Robert did."

I nod my head. "I know, bud. I'm so sorry."

I reach over to find the remote and change the channel, but the damage has been done. How often does Kamau think of this? Did Robert's abuse contribute to the fall? Is it a coincidence that shortly after Kamau told me what happened he jumped from the upper level of a parking structure? Kamau remembers nothing about the leap he took. But why was one of the first things he said: "What about Robert?"

What the hell about Robert?

I don't know any more than I did before.

52

Behavioral Health

After two months out of work, not counting a brief, disastrous stint at a daycare center, I know it's time to get a job, and I know what I want to be, a Patient Safety Companion, or sitter. I think I will be able to give back for the hundreds of hours that sitters have watched over my boy. I imagine myself at Chandler, sitting beside someone like Kamau, who has been in a terrible accident. This is not the case. I do get to sit with people like Kamau, only they are severely mentally ill, and a danger to themselves.

In my interview, Karen Carroll, the Director of Nursing on the Behavioral Health unit at University of Kentucky Good Samaritan Hospital, tells me that if hired I will sit with the difficult patients. They are not mere fall risks. These are patients who are violent, actively suicidal, or psychotic and inappropriate.

She shows me the unit, and I try to keep up. Karen is a tall, wiry woman with an athletic build, blonde hair, and a look that makes it hard to determine her age. She strides purposefully down the hall, familiar to me, as I'd walked through it before to take Kamau to the kids' unit.

The faces I pass look exhausted, their features shadowed with the same resigned desperation that mirrors my own face. I envy them a bed to sleep in a few days away from all their cares and woes, and then I think, *What the hell, Claudia? You're identifying with the mentally ill patients during your interview. Are you crazy?* And because crazy people dialogue with themselves and answer themselves, I said, *Why, yes, I am crazy, and I've wanted to scream bloody, freaking murder for the past two months.* But I mention none of this to Karen. I do tell her about Kamau, however—his mental illness, accident, and that I need a flexible schedule. She tells me if I'm hired I can call in on the days I can work, an amazing perk. Sitters, she says, are almost always needed.

A few days later, she offers me the job. This is a terrible decision. I have no business working with mentally ill people right now, but here I am, crazy, on the Behavioral Health Unit, but not the patient.

53

It's Not About Me

My first day on the job I get in trouble. I am sitting with a suicidal man. He is pleasant, cooperative, and active. This is not a patient who will stay in his room all day feeling sorry for himself. He is tall, like a basketball player, and thin, and I have to hustle to keep up with him. I shadow his every move, and am able to follow him into the Day Room where he interacts with other patients.

During snack time, I listen to a sunken-faced woman who attempted suicide by overdosing. She talks about giving up. I am a caretaker. A habitual patcher-upper, I'm not surprised when I hear Kamau's story come flying out of my mouth, loudly, a lesson in perseverance, and how you can get through anything if you're still breathing.

A nurse pulls me to the side. "You can't do that," she says. "You can't tell them anything personal. This is not about you."

This is a revelation. Everything has been about me. Me and Kamau. What happened to us is all I think about. It's most of what I talk about.

She tells Karen that I got personal with a patient. Karen doesn't call me on it this time, but this incident will be remembered and brought to my attention later, mostly because it won't be the last time I do it.

54

Cardinal Hill

July finds me precariously employed. Kamau is released from Chandler to Cardinal Hill, a rehab facility. He is placed on a brain injury unit, and his trach tube is removed. The blunt force trauma to his head when he fell face first jarred his brain as his face slammed against the concrete, then bounced hard on the surface of the back of his skull. Despite his progress, Kamau is very thin and weak. He is not yet steady on his feet, and his thinking darkens and clouds like a storm coming. He is ten days from coming home.

I am in the room with Kamau. He is standing in front of the mirror on his own. His sitter excuses herself to take a quick break. Kamau searches the reflection he sees in the bathroom mirror. He has lost thirty pounds from an already lean frame, and looks gaunt. His left cheek sticks out unnaturally wider than the right. He is not as pretty as he used to be. A long scar meanders across his forehead, and scars slash his chin and jaw where surgeons went in to fix him. Many of his teeth are missing, and his mouth is still wired shut, which makes him drool.

When I say drool, I don't mean a thin line of saliva glazing his chin. A constant stream of slobber slides out of his mouth and will fall all the way down to the floor if we don't stop it. He has to keep a towel in one hand to wipe at it. But this never seems to disturb him. Almost nothing appears to bother him now.

"What do you think when you see yourself now?" I ask him.

He pauses for a moment. "I think, 'Who is this guy? What is he up to?'"

I expected a soap opera of self-pity, and find him both curious and quite possibly eager for a new adventure. Yes, he's had his fearful days. Who wouldn't in his predicament? Mostly he's been admirably brave, and I'm proud of him.

Part Three

55

Home

On the day Kamau is released, he sits outside in a lawn chair asking for a cigarette. He's dying to smoke. The kid still drools an impressive, unbroken line of spittle five feet from mouth to ground from his still wired shut mouth. He can drink and eat soft foods with the wiring, but he wants a cig.

"No," I say, always the buzzkill. "The doctor says they're bad for your healing brain."

"Aww, Mom, just one." But I'm adamant. So, he sits by the rose bushes sulking, looking so beautiful and alive—Kamau is ALIVE—that I'm overcome with emotion. I want to capture the moment, him sitting right there in the welcoming sun, with his U.K. T-shirt on, looking like everything is going to be all right, looking like hope itself, looking like a miracle. I grab my iPhone and snap a picture. Every time I look at it, him wide eyed and a little uncertain, I think, *This is what anything is possible looks like.*

56

The Puppy

My birthday is coming up, and Carly tells me a story. I wasn't raised by our parents, but rather, by our great aunt. I missed these little gems about my siblings Carly knows so well.

She tells me that when she was a little girl, on one of her birthdays, she wanted a puppy. How she waited for the promised furry present, but when her birthday arrived, no puppy. She was inconsolable, and henceforth referred to that day as the No Puppy Birthday. After that, every awful birthday was a No Puppy Birthday. She is determined that I will get a puppy, metaphorically, of course.

This gets me thinking, and now I want a puppy, a real puppy. I want a pug, so I ask my neighbor, Remy, who just happens to rescue animals, if they have a pug puppy available, and will wonders cease? They do! I speak with the woman fostering the little guy, and she agrees to bring him over to meet us.

The puppy is a wild thing. He runs circles around my legs and yips at me. He zooms around the yard, and his enviable energy terrifies me.

"He's like a toddler," his foster mom says. "Think of having a new two-year-old in the house. That's what it will be like."

I cannot imagine a two-year-old in the house.

He's so cute, but Kamau is my toddler. I fluff his pillows at night and kiss his cheek. I tell him about my vision of him being one hundred percent. I come to his every call. I watch his moves as he paces the floor, circling the house over and over. I clean up his drool using every towel in the house. I already have a puppy.

"Thanks," I tell the woman. "I don't think I can handle him and my son."

"No problem," she tells me. "We want him to go to the right home."

I think about Kamau, and how unequipped I feel to care for him. I'm not even sure he's in the right home, but I hope so.

That's all I've got.

57

Scene of the Accident

Kamau insists that he wants to go the top of the parking structure he jumped from. I try for days to talk him out of this visit to the scene of the accident, but he's convinced it may give him answers as to why he jumped. One brilliantly fine August afternoon, four months after the fall, we walk in the sun washed day to the corner of Short and Broadway. Upon arrival I begin to hyperventilate. Kamau is calm personified. He strides to the elevator with me slogging behind him, doing whatever overcooked pasta would do if it could attempt some semblance of walking. He waits for me, a mouth-breathing, limp noodle nearly passed out, to enter the elevator. When I'm finally inside, he presses 'six.' That's a long way up. And a long way down. It takes both forever and no time for us to arrive at the top level.

Kamau doesn't seem to notice that I'm having a full-blown panic attack. He goes straight to the edge of the roof while I chant "OhmyGodohmyGodohmyGodohmyGod," what feels like several thousand times, but may have only been twice.

"I'm really uncomfortable up here," I say, ready to vomit.

"I used to come up here all the time," Kamau says. He heads over to the undersized wall he had to have jumped from, and peers over the edge. "I wonder what I was thinking. Why I would do that?"

I follow him in an attempt at being supportive, and try to peek over the edge myself. I want to faint. "OhmyGodohmyGodohmyGod." This distance, from here to the ground, is what almost killed us.

Now, I'm trying not to throw up and or lose consciousness. I skitter away from my pondering child and his frightening inquiries, screeching, "Can we please get away from here?"

Kamau stands at the wall, looking for answers that were knocked out of his head in the fall. I don't think he'll ever find them. He shakes his head, then walks over to me, links his arm in mine, and we leave. We are no wiser now than we were when we came.

58

Cognitive Functioning

Kamau's outpatient occupational therapy involves taking a number of tests that measure his cognitive functioning. In one such test, he is given a list of animals to remember in chronological order.

Cat
Mouse
Dog
Fish
Aardvark
Giraffe
Tiger

Kamau gets every answer right. I, on the other hand, get two right.

The person with the brain injury nails this test, and I profoundly fail it. *Something is wrong with my brain,* I think. *I'm dying. I have a tumor. That's why I feel so bad. Or my brain is deteriorating. I have Alzheimer's. I'm going to waste away.*

To test my theory, I slyly try a few more tests Kamau passes with ease. I fail them all.

Later, I make a doctor's appointment. She doesn't order any tests. She asks how I am sleeping. Fitfully. And if I am under stress. When am I not? Then she diagnoses me with overwhelm.

I could have diagnosed myself with that, I think. *Medical school, I missed my calling.*

59

A Conversation

Two unmistakable facts remain despite all that has happened:
One: I am still in love with Ken, my husband, and
Two: Ken blames me for what happened to Kamau.
I want Ken to move back home, but first we need to have a conversation.

Me: You left me alone to deal with all this.
Ken: You let him go down.
Me: I don't pass out mental illnesses; otherwise, I would have skipped me and Kamau.
Ken: (…)
Me: Come back home. I need you.
Ken: Things have to be different.
Me: They will be.

60

Fisticuffs

Things are definitely different now that Ken is back home. Kamau is a tempest, and Ken keeps getting caught in the bad weather. This boy, who is all sweetness to me, is churlish and sullen with his father. Then insolent. Ken deals with Kamau's smart mouth by snatching him up with both fists, and the two begin to push and hit each other.

I don't understand this. Doesn't Ken get that Kamau has a brain injury, that the damage to his frontal lobe affects his behavior? Kamau can be irritable. Impulsive. Can't Ken in turn offer him patience and kindness?

Carly and I wedge between them, a boy and his father, brawling like they're in a bar.

Ken tells me their fractured relationship is all my fault for coddling him.

"You never let me discipline him," he says.

He's right. I didn't let him do this, because I've never believed that was discipline. I still don't.

61

Man of the House

Carly moves out soon after Ken arrives. The impatiens die. The garden perishes of neglect, all but the roses. Carly says she doesn't feel right being here. Ken is the man of the house, and his presences negates the need for hers. Now it seems like all he does to assert his authority is fight with Kamau.

One day I find him and Kamau wrestling in the middle of the living room floor. It is not friendly roughhousing. Kamau has stolen weed from Ken, and Ken has turned the confrontation physical. Kamau has reacted. Now Aziza, hysterical, is beating on Kamau's back, demanding that he get off her dad. The scene is so familiar I ache. It is my own childhood, the violence, my screaming reaction. My mother's impotence against the chaos. All over again.

I manage to pull Kamau off Ken in order to scream at Ken.

"What's wrong with you? You should know better."

"That's why I left," he yells. "You don't let me be a man."

I don't give Kamau a pass for this fight either. Much of his conduct is learned behavior, not brain injury related acting out, but his brain influences his behavior, and that should always be taken into account. I think Ken should be the bigger man. He thinks Kamau should be a boy he can handle with the old school rod of correction.

No matter how he tries to work it, Kamau is not seven-years-old. Physical altercations won't work. It's a mess that keeps getting messier.

62

Nineteen

On his birthday, April 1st, twenty-six days shy of a year after he swooped from the top of a six story parking structure, Kamau loses his Medicaid insurance. There are no other benefits for him at this time. Lawyers are still fighting the Social Security Adminisitration for us.

This is no April Fool's day joke. There's nothing funny about a mentally ill person without healthcare coverage. Kamau is completely vulnerable.

I am terrified. Kamau shrugs it off, as if it's a small technicality, too sick to realize what this really means.

63

Micah

I dread the days at work that I have to sit with Micah. He's a teenager with a psychotic disorder precipitated by drug use. In other words, Micah is my nightmare.

I listen to the other sitters complain about him. Micah can be violent. Micah can be inappropriate. Micah makes sitters want to quit their jobs. Today, Micah demands a different sitter, and I'm the last option.

I trudge to the kid's unit like I'm in a funeral procession, and Micah looks me over like I'm prey. He's African American, and I'm hoping my age, plump body, and caramel-colored skin will remind him of a kindly old auntie, and he will go easy on me. Then I realize he has a psychotic disorder. While some of his issues are behavioral, most of them are not.

Micah is king of the unit. He walks the hallway like he owns it and asks for things I cannot give him: snacks and drinks when it isn't time to pass them out. He goes into the fridge anyway and heists cartons of juice, and I do not stop him. I think about Kamau, and the possibility of him smoking a single joint and ending up back here. I see him terrorizing sitters, abandoning comforting structure, and wreaking havoc on set schedules.

Micah goes to his room, and I'm behind him like I'm the back of his shirt. He crawls into his bed, and I sit in the chair at his desk. Then he places his hands in his pants and fiercely masturbates. My polite pleas for him to stop go unheeded.

A painful vision of Kamau disorients me. I see him abandoned to the whims of his damaged brain without thought to decorum. Frontal lobe injuries often come with sexual acting out. Once I asked Kamau during his recovery if he wanted something. He asked me if I could get him a blow job. Sitting here, I imagine Micah is my son. My horrifying son, the one I cannot stop from masturbating in front of me. I am ready to run screaming from the room when Micah leaps up from the bed and strips completely naked.

I am stunned. "My eyes! My eyes!" I yell. I saw a wide and swirly-eyed character say that line in a Sponge Bob movie, and it comes to me now, as if this child has blinded me with his raw butt. The staff rushes to my aid to realize the only thing that Micah has done to me is bare his ass. They tell him to put his clothes back on, and probably note that I am the worst sitter the unit has ever seen.

Interestingly enough, the next time Micah needs a sitter, he asks for me. He likes me. The people on the kid's unit think I'm good for him. They request me, too. Begrudgingly, I go.

64

In the Meantime

I realize one late Summer morning that our family has plodded our way into "the mean time," that liminal place that began with Kamau's first signs of mental illness, and will end in a tenuous future which, right now, we can't readily conceptualize. In this threshold to whatever will come after, we rise and work, love and fight, sleep and rise, then repeat.

65

College

Kamau has no work of his own, and is unambiguously resistant to volunteering anywhere, especially at The Participation Station, a peer ran support program for those with mental illness. Other than pacing the paint off our yellow studio floor with his anxious stalking the room, Kamau is terminally bored. I feel like I have to find him something for him to do, but what that is eludes me.

He comes to me one afternoon with a plan. Kamau is always making plans, few of which work out.

"Ma, I want to go to college. I want to study film at BCTC. Can I take GED classes so I can finish my highschool stuff?" Greedy to move forward with his life, enthusiasm shines in his round, brown eyes.

Kamau showed an interest in Bluegrass Community and Technical College's Filmaking Certificate program even before the accident that compromised his brain. Even before he followed the birds, and walked around as naked as Adam in the Garden.

Ken is an artist. I'm a writer. We've always supported our children's creative dreams, but the truth of the matter is, Ken and I don't think Kamau is ready for school. Delusions still linger in his often troubled mind, but I don't feel there's much I can do to dissuade him. He wants to try to attend, and we need to allow him to grow up, and out from under the quivering wings of our protection.

"There's a phone number I see on a big sign when I drive downtown," I say. "It's for a GED program I think is free. I'll jot it down and you can call this week."

He rewards my reluctant approval with a big, toothless grin.

A few days later, Kamau makes his first inquiry. A pre-test is required, that will determine which classes he needs to take to brush up on his skills before the final test. He's granted permission to test with the next group of prospective program participants.

A week later, from my little black sofa, I watch Kamau bound out the front door to go downtown like he's off to see the Wizard of Oz for a brain. I sit there, my hands clasped in my lap, wondering how the hell a kid with a psychotic disorder is going to succeed in a classroom.

Kamau returns home hours later with good news. He's passed the pre-test. His score is so high that he doesn't have to take the classes, afterall. He squuezes me into an excited hug, and in his gangly arms I stand corrected.

66

Graduation

Kamau's GED completion program doesn't just have him take a test and wait for a certificate to come in the mail. They go BIG. There is a cap and gown graduation ceremony to reward the students for their hard work, and I am all about that life.

I think I'm more excited by this than Kamau is. I want to do it all: graduation pictures, announcements, a party, but all he says is, "Ma, chill."

On his graduation day, I'm barely able to contain myself. I can't remember when I've been so happy. He may have denied me a studio photographer shoot, but my iPhone will not be denied. I snap pictures of him by the rose bush outside our little yellow ranch house. Instead of the goofy toothless grin I'm used to, he crosses his arms, and trains his brooding eyes on me, like this whole GED thing has grown him up, and he's too cool to smile.

The commencement exercise takes place one year to the day that Kamau was released from Cardinal Hill. It's so damned beautiful. It's brutiful, the tender combination of the brutal and beautiful writer Glennon Doyle writes about. The speakers unashamedly share the hardships that denied them their initial highschool success, and they celebrate with stories the triumps that brought them to the stage today. Their words inspire and challenge me, and as I shoot pictures of the back of Kamau's graduation capped head. I have the strongest sense that we are going to be just fine.

Afterward, at the reception, I ask Ken to take a photo of Kamau and I. It will be the first picture we've taken together since our hospital room selfies. Every time I see this picture, a mother beaming with pride, standing next to the boy who not only lived, but did this incredible thing that I didn't think was possible, I caption it in my heart with, "But God." As in, we fell down and shattered into pieces, *but God* saw fit to lift us up, healing body and soul, with his strong, but gentle hands.

67

Healing

When Kamau enrolls at BCTC, the film program welcomes him, but he grows sicker by the day. His grandiosity swells as September wanes. Kamau argues with his professor, sure he knows more than she does. He is disruptive, and the finished work he brings home could be decoded by cryptanalysis. I can only imagine what his teacher thinks when she reads his papers.

An altercation involving a girl in his class, who Kamau says another young man was harassing, ends when Kamau threatens him with his shoe. The school administration considers this a terroristic threat, and Kamau is expelled from the program, unable to attend any classes at BCTC for a year. I grieve this loss with him, and wonder if he will ever have the creative life he craves, and that I covet for him.

So many artists are touched by the luminous flames of bipolar disorder. Yet, they excel in music, film, literature, and visual art. Sometimes they just kick ass in the simple, but shining lives they craft for themselves. Without a doubt bipolar artists are familiar with darkness, but roused from their death-like depressive slumbers, the achingly brilliant days return as surely as the tide.

In less than a week Kamau is admitted to the psychiatric hospital for a manic episode. We are not yet whole; we're healing.

68

Florence Avenue

At the end of August of 2013, my friend Lisa's husband Will meets with me in a local Starbucks. He and Lisa are divorcing. In the proceedings,Will is awarded the house that I rent from them, that Lisa so generously ignores my late, partial, and sometimes non-existent rent payments for. We sit at the small table, over-priced coffees in front of us. I am expecting Will to say that we will have to be more consistent in our rent payments, or that he's raising the rent. The news is worse. He tells me he is broke and has to sell the house. He cries.

My family moved to Kentucky to be a part of an intentional Christian community. We would "do life" with the Samsons and the corporeal works of mercy. For awhile we were magnificent. We ate meals together, prayed the Liturgy of hours, and in whatever way we could, became the merciful hands and feet of Jesus to whomever God would send our way. Our kids would grow up together. We were boots on the ground all in.

That was over now: Will's dream of living in grace-filled community with us, and mine. I place my hand on his and say to him that it's okay. Somehow, we will be all right. I'm not sure we will, but I tell myself this is true to keep from weeping and gnashing my teeth, surrounded by hipsters, clacking on their laptops and sipping coffees with names I would never remember.

69

Boys in the Hood

In October, we move to "the hood." Florence Avenue is one of the most violent streets in Lexington. When I tell my friend Iris from work where I'll be living, she replies, "Oh, Lord. I'm gonna pray you outta there." A woman from Carly's Bible study class, where I teach arts and crafts (when I show up) says, "Be careful on Florence."

Kamau has never met a stranger, and his brain injury makes him even more open, unmindful of the potential for harm. He walks down to the hottest trap house on the block, where one can see drug transactions take place out in the open, and I'm aghast that there he makes friends.

Not all these young people sell drugs, but some do. And not all of them know how to take Kamau. They can tell something is wrong with him, but it's hard to determine what, so they label him as crazy. The meaner kids in the crowd taunt him. They hit him, mostly in the face, and he literally runs away, bolting from the conflict. Kamau spends hours away from home. I have no idea they're assaulting him regularly.

Once he came home with broken glasses.

"What happened, Kamau?"

"One of the guys hit me in the face."

"Hard enough to break your glasses?"

"We were just messing around."

I don't think Kamau can discern the difference between horseplay with your boys and abuse by bullies. Or worse, he can tell, but keeps going back to the bullies anyway.

All of Kamau's old friends have vanished like vapors. Kamau chases after their scent, but they slip away. They lost the Kamau they knew at bottom of the parking structure. Soon their tears stop flowing, and the new Kamau, desperately seeking marijuana and irritating them with his impulsivity and strangeness, took his place. This Kamau wears their patience thin.

Now, the boys in the neighborhood up their ante. One Autumn day Jermaine pulls a gun on Kamau. It won't be the last time. By late Fall, a drive-by shooting happens at the trap house two duplexes down from us. Three people are shot.

Kamau's psychosis is constant, but low grade, not enough for him to be hospitalized for. I learn that your mentally ill people are *your* problem. There are few long-term solutions.

"I have to fight the whole world, Mom."

"What do you mean?"

"Everybody wants to fight me. I have to go to war with the world. I need to gather an army. I'm going to lose an eye, but..."

"Kamau, no. You don't have to fight anybody."

"I have to fight everybody."

Violence and death entangle his thoughts. I am afraid for my son. Sometimes, I am afraid *of* my son.

70

Family Annihilator

Kamau tells me he will kill our whole family. He is especially angry at Ken, but he will kill all of us. He will kill me.

I am tired. Too much has gone on, and I handle most of it, but I can't deal with much more.

"Nobody that came out of my womb is killing me. Do you hear me, boy? You will not be killing me."

I march him to my car to drive him to Eastern State Hospital. His sister Abbie goes with me. On the way, Kamau repeatedly tries to open the car door and we scramble to keep him safe in our vehicle. It is a harrowing ride, but we finally arrive and get him inside. After an hour, an intake nurse comes out and speaks to me. She tells me that even though I've made it clear that Kamau has threatened the family, and posed a danger to himself by trying to jump out of a moving car, Kamau does not meet criteria for admission.

What that the hell?

Abbie and I collect our mentally ill person, take another frightening drive to Good Samaritan Hospital to the unit, and they admit Kamau without hesitation. I will not be able to work on the adult unit while he is a patient, but I know he will be taken care of, and for a second or two, I will be able to breathe.

71

Altruistic Healer

Whenever something happens to Kamau, I call Dr. Glaser. He checks on him, writes letters to the court, advises—whatever needs to be done. In the period of time in which Kamau has no health insurance, and prior to Kamau receiving Social Security Disability benefits, Dr. Glaser kindly sees Kamau after hours on his own time. We trudge into the office, and Dr. Glaser is as affable as ever, even after seeing patients all day. After he speaks with Kamau, he talks to me about my boy, and then he asks about me. These little "sessions" with Dr. Glaser sustain me.

Sometimes, he gives me samples of antidepressants, which I desperately need. I have no health insurance either. When they work, he writes me a prescription, something I can get from the four-dollar list of medications at Walmart. Somehow, in all the madness, this amazing, highly regarded child psychiatrist becomes my doctor, too.

72

Scream

I am on the kid's unit. The staff has grown used to me. I have curbed my tendency to tell personal stories, and spend more time listening to patients than talking to them. I'm better at my job. Sometimes, I'm good at it. Often, especially on the kid's side, they ask for me.

Today, Wendy, the same nurse who admitted Kamau for his first hospitalization, and I are in the Day Room. I've talked about Kamau with her dozens of times, just as she's talked about her quadriplegic husband Tom with me. These are our stories, the defining tales that have shaped our lives.

It is mandatory room time for the kids, and Wendy and I get a few moments away from them to commiserate.

"Sometimes, I just want to go somewhere and scream and scream, Wendy."

"Go somewhere and scream."

"I can't," I say.

"I understand," she says. "This is what we've got."

I nod my head. She really does understand.

73

Avery

Kamau leaves the hospital, a little more clear-headed, but not a lot. There is little long-term help available for Kamau. So far, we've been denied Social Security Disability benefits twice and have had to get a lawyer. I continue to work regularly on the kid's side, in a new position opened up called a Hallway Monitor, whose main job is to keep children out of each other's rooms.

Avery comes one afternoon. She is a quiet, pretty twelve-year-old who should be more concerned about studying, kindness club meetings, and her crush than about suicidal thoughts, but here she is. Most of the kids on our unit have overdosed. Avery is no exception. Their reasons are varied: school stress, breakups, their mom taking away their iPhone. Avery's reason for attempting suicide is different. She has revealed that a family member sexually abused her. And her mother did nothing.

Avery's disclosure is not readily apparent. After a few disturbing hints, our social worker Carla coaxes the story out of her. Child Protective Services is notified, and Avery is given a choice: will she testify against the person who hurt her?

She will.

Brave girl, I think. *Brave, brave girl.*

74

The Nature Conservancy

Lumumba has spent the night with us, a respite from his bachelor pad. He wakes me up early on this Sunday morning.

"Mom, Kamau has someone's car. He's driving it around."

I roll back over to go back to sleep.

"Mom! Wake up! He's sick. He has someone's car."

Wait a minute. He has someone's car? Kamau doesn't have a driver's license. He's barely had driving lessons. Who would give him a car? I'm awake now, but because my joints are stiff in the morning, I can't just leap out of bed. I shout to Lumumba, "Get him! Call him for me."

Mumba rushes out of the room to get his brother before he leaves in God only knows whose vehicle again, and a few minutes later Kamau bounces into my room. I sit up in the bed.

"Mom," he says. "I got a job. They let me have a car and everything."

"Who gave you a job?"

"The Nature Conservancy."

"Who?"

Then he slows down and speaks to me like I'm stupid. "The. Nay. Tchure. Conserve. Vancy." He dangles the keychain with the logo in front of my face. It says "The Nature Conservancy."

"Kamau...."

"I gotta go, Mom."

"Wait!"

But he's too fast. Before I can get out of bed he's out of the house and driving on the streets of Lexington.

I'm terrified. I know no one has given my delusional child a job and company car. Not only do I fear for Kamau's safety, but for other drivers, too. I throw some clothes on, grab my keys and purse, and take off, trying to figure out where he'd go joy riding to. I look all around downtown, and don't spot the white SUV Lumumba described. Finally, I pick up Carly, and we drive around some more.

Then, it occurs to me. Maybe Kamau went to "work." Carly does an internet search on her phone for the Nature Conservancy, and we rush over to Woodland Street on the other side of downtown, hoping to find him.

When we arrive at the stately old Victorian house where the Nature Conservancy's office is located, we see a white SUV with the company logo on the side. A side window to the house is broken, and shards of glass lie on the grass. Carly and I step out of the car and look around. We approach the entrance hesitantly. It's early, but people are milling about. They make me nervous. The Nature Conservancy is obviously closed on Sunday. So what are the two distressed-looking Black women doing at the door? We certainly aren't Jehovah's witnesses. Not the way we're dressed in our *throw something on, anything, Kamau is psychotic and on the loose* clothes.

I knock, but there's no answer. Knock again. Still nothing. Then I call his name.

"Kamau! Kamau!"

He answers the door of the large Victorian house where The Nature Conservancy resides. "Mom! This is my new job. Do you want me to show you around?"

I'm scared. I think the White people milling about are going to call the police on the suspicious looking Black folks any moment, and not only will we all be arrested, Kamau will resist arrest because he thinks he works here, and we will all be tragically misunderstood and killed by a police force hostile to Black people. In my imagination, we are already dead.

"Can you just come on out, baby?" I say, my voice tremulous.

Kamau is wearing a denim button-down shirt with a Nature Conservancy logo on it that he must have found inside. I have to admit, when he goes psychotic, he commits. He truly believes he works there. Carly tries to reason with him.

"Why don't you go for a ride with us?"

Sunlight blankets the day in light and warmth. More people come outside to enjoy its beauty. My anxiety rises with every new person I see who has emerged from their pricey home.

"Do you want some soda or a snack?" Kamau asks.

"No. We want you to come with us," Carly urges.

"Let me take you to breakfast," I say. This kid never says no to food.

Breakfast is the magic word. Kamau locks up his delusional place of business, puts keys that don't belong to him in his pocket, and gets in my car, while Carly and I try not to draw attention to ourselves by being two middle-aged Black women in this neighborhood. I work hard not to burn rubber pealing out of the driveway, while hyperventilating all the way to McDonald's for cheap breakfast because I did say I'd buy some. Fortunately, Good Sam is across the street from Mickey D's. Carly and I get a sausage McMuffin for Kamau, and drive right to the hospital. It takes a lot of convincing to get him to go inside, and when he finally does, he won't talk to a doctor. I rush upstairs to the Behavioral Health Unit for help.

Iris sees me first. I look wild-eyed, Don King-haired and in clothes that don't match.

"What's wrong?" she says.

"It's Kamau. He broke into the Nature Conservancy. He thinks he works there. He's psychotic."

Wendy is working on the adult side today. She stops and folds me into a fierce, snap-out-of-it hug that is as effective as a slap in the face. I pull myself together as she asks for details.

"Where is he?"

"He's downstairs. He won't talk to the doctor."

"Everything is going to be okay," she says, with the kind of brisk authority nurses are famous for. We send another friend, Ashley, a Mental Health Associate on the unit working on her master's degree in psychology downstairs to talk to him. She convinces him to speak to a doctor. Kamau is over eighteen, and I have no legal right to commit him without petitioning the court first, but the hospital will do this automatically if they admit him. I just need him to willingly sign himself in first.

The mental health system is complicated. Either you meet criteria for involuntary admission—you're at risk to harm yourself or others—or you check yourself in. It is not easy to get a floridly psychotic person to do anything, especially if they aren't trying to hurt anyone, including themselves. We manage to get Kamau admitted, and I explain what's going on to the intake nurse.

She tells me I have to call the police and report that Kamau broke into the Nature Conservancy. If I don't call, the hospital will, and Kamau will be arrested on the spot. If I call, he can remain in the hospital, and the case will most likely be thrown out of court. I ask for a phone.

For the second time, I have to deal with Kamau and a criminal charge. I wonder what his life will be like when I'm not around to make the call to keep him out of jail.

75

From the Police Report

Post-Arrest Complaint
Burglary 3rd Degree. Receiving stolen property.

*S*ubject admitted to breaking into "The Nature Conservancy." He advised that he was trying to get inside to work. The suspect does not work or reside at the business. Suspect admitted to taking car keys and driving one of the business cars. He has two sets of keys to vehicles belonging to the business.

76

Iris

Iris is the clerk on the Behavioral Health Unit. She survived the death of her son who was murdered. Now plagued by health concerns, Iris has gained custody of her young grandchildren, and I often inquire about her and them, the way she asks about me and Kamau. Today, I am anxious about Kamau's future. It is the rare day I see nothing for him but misery and pain, and severe mental illness. I ask her, "Do you think it would be better for God to take someone and spare their suffering, or allow them to stay and let them keep going through horrible things?"

Iris sees right through my question. "I'd rather have him. At least you have your son. I don't have mine. I don't get to look at him, or touch him, or hold him. You can do that."

I feel like a monster for allowing myself to think such a thought for even a moment, and I ask God to forgive me for my lapse. But I'm human. I just want his suffering to stop.

77

Jermaine

Kamau is in the hospital for five days, just long enough to stabilize him. He is not completely himself. Delusions cling to him, but he recognizes that they're delusions now. When he comes home, he continues to hang out with the neighborhood boys, who continue to bully him. Jermaine pulls a gun on him again, Kamau tells me. This weighs heavily on me when I'm at work one morning.

We're in Recreation Therapy, and the kids have free time. There are few of them, and they're all occupied, so we staff people, friends all, can talk.

I tell the gang the problem. "I've decided to just go down there and confront Jermaine. I mean, he hasn't done anything, really, but wave a gun around. I'm not even sure it's loaded. Maybe I can reason with him."

My friends unanimously said no.

"You don't know what this kid will do," Ashley says, shaking her pretty head.

Adam agrees. "Kids aren't like they used to be. You can't always reason with them, and you definitely can't scare some of them. It could be extremely dangerous."

So, I decide not to go. But if Jermaine could be a danger to me, what about to my son? Maybe it isn't posturing with an unloaded gun like Kamau said. I go to our unit's social worker Barb. She is so good-natured, kind and always accessible, both to patients and coworkers. "I've got to get Kamau off of Florence Ave," I tell her. "Somebody may just kill him if I don't. Please help me."

"I'll make some calls," Barb says.

A former Good Sam employee, Lindsey Jasinski, is in charge of opening an Acquired Brain Injury unit at Eastern State Hospital. It's a long-term care program with a four to six-month residency. She will talk to Lindsey. Maybe there is something she can do.

Those of us who pray do, to this end. We don't know yet that in a few years Jermaine will use that gun and murder a man not much older than Kamau, but the possibility of such senseless violence is ever-present. Wisely, we don't trust the situation.

78

Avery's Mom

By now I work on the kid's unit almost all the time. In the Spring of 2013, Avery returns to the unit. She is a little more grown up, almost thirteen now, more confident, and more beautiful. She is still in the kindness club.

Avery is having a difficult time at home, and feeling suicidal once again, but she has not acted on it this time, a remarkable improvement. She had testified against her family member, and this person has gone to prison. After she told her story, other family members came forward with their stories of how they, too, had been molested by the same person. Apparently, this individual blazed through generations hurting children. Decades of secrets were now being spoken aloud. Survivor's plaintive cries were being heard.

One afternoon, I sit across from Avery. The hallway is quiet. Most kids are in their rooms.

"Avery, what is the one thing you wish would have happened in your abuse case?"

"I wish my mother had done something when I told her what happened."

I nod. Suddenly, I have an answer to Kamau's question, "What about Robert?"

Do something. Now.

79

Email

After my talk with Avery, I can hardly concentrate at work. I spend every spare moment drafting an email to the Archbishop of the Eastern Orthodox Episcopate in Detroit. I spare no detail about Robert's abuse, his grooming of Kamau by buying him things we couldn't afford, his showing him pornography and facilitating a precocious sexual awakening, and finally touching him. I tell about the fall, and the question (What about Robert?) that comes when Kamau can finally talk. When I am done I press send, and call the Detroit Police. They tell me Kamau is eighteen-years-old. I cannot call for him. This is something Kamau will have to do himself. Another battle for me has begun.

80

The Police

I ask Kamau if he will call the police to report what Robert has done. He flatly refuses, despite my pleading.

81

Mama's Boy

Sometimes my begging like a rhythm and blues singer (please, please, baby, please) actually works. After a few weeks of my imploring, Kamau agrees to speak with the police. He is, after all, a mama's boy. The Detroit Police advise us to take him to the Lexington Police to make a statement. Ken takes Kamau to the station, where his statement is videotaped. His dad is not allowed to be present for the taping, but Kamau gets through it. When he's done, Ken and I tell him how proud we are of him. At home we prepare for the long process of finding justice. It isn't like it is on *Law and Order: Special Victims Unit*. The players aren't glamorous, the work is tedious, and the case will take a hell of a lot longer than fifty minutes without commercial breaks.

82

Sometimes

I watch Kamau pace up and down the hall, stopping only to go outside and have a cigarette, or say some absurdist funny thing to me that never fails to make me laugh for the sheer wackiness of it. He writes a Facebook status on his cryptic page that says, "The self-evident exploding turtle theory." And that's it. It makes me smile, because I know Kamau said things like this even before he became ill. He's just a sweet weirdo.

Sometimes my heart flares up like flame when I look at him. I love him so.

Don't let anybody hurt him before I can get help, I pray. *Please God, don't let anyone hurt him. He's been hurt enough.*

I pray it over and over.

83

Eastern State

Just as Kamau's Social Security Disability comes through, so does a bed on Lindsey's Acquired Brain Injury Unit. Kamau is one of the first residents. He's a model patient and his cognitive functions, already impressive for what happened to him, improves dramatically. On the ABI unit, Kamau's IQ, diminished after the fall, increases and his memory improves with therapy. He learns to cook and make a budget. He goes on field trips and makes art.

When he is discharged five months later, he moves next door to Central Kentucky Recovery Center. With more freedom comes more struggle for Kamau. He finds ways to get marijuana, and this drives me insane. On more than one occasion, his residency and CKRC is jeopardized, but he always vows to change and stop the drug use. Kamau stays at CKRC for five months, then moves on to his own apartment with wrap-around services in place. A therapist visits him in his home, a nurse, and he has a social worker. There is peer support for him and rides to appointments. Their goal is to give Kamau some independence from me. I'm grateful for this. I need the break, and I want Kamau to be more responsible. I'm always thinking about, what if I die? What's going to happen to Kamau? These angels give me hope that Kamau will be all right should I suddenly not be around to help him.

84

Investigation

When I report Robert to the Episcopate in Detroit, the Orthodox Church in America's offices in New York is informed. They gather a team together, consisting of a priest, a proto-deacon, and a former police officer who specialized in sex crimes to investigate my allegation. The three men come to our duplex on Florence. They sit at the kitchen table with Kamau, Ken and me, and fire questions at us. Did I know anything about Robert? Did I allow Kamau to go off alone with him? Once again, I feel like I am up for the worst mother in the world award. Finally, I say to the men, "I wanted God in my life. I went to church. I asked the priest if Robert could be trusted to be a good Godfather. He seemed to be a righteous man. I believed the priest when he said he was." There is little comfort in this, but I have to tell myself I meant my child no harm. I wanted him to know God.

85

Sex Offender

I'm at the hospital one night, in the emergency room. I'm having chest pains. Stress is killing me, and for once I can't ignore myself. Even in my vulnerable condition I'm thinking of Kamau. I wonder if Robert is a registered sex offender. Surely not. He'd never be allowed to be an altar server, such a visible position in the Eastern Orthodox Church, or around children, if he were. On a whim I check the Michigan Sex Offender Registry. Robert has been on there since the freakin' nineties. He has been active for years, meaning he had to report in on a regular basis. He knew he was not allowed to be involved with a child when he agreed to be Kamau's Godfather. I find this out in two minutes. I only wished I had checked the sex offender registry when vetting him as a Godfather instead of just asking our parish priest.

I alert the Archbishop of Robert's sex offender status, and he is removed from all positions in the church. When the team who investigated my allegations finish their work, Kamau is found to be believable. Robert, the sex offender, is found to be deceptive. If only the criminal case wrapped up as quickly.

86

Dean

One afternoon I get a Facebook Message from a friend from the Orthodox Church we attended. He sends a picture to me for old time's sake. Robert is in the picture. I write to him.

"Oh, Dean. You don't know, do you?"

"Know what?"

"Robert was showing Kamau pornography for years. He sexually assaulted him."

Dean is shocked. Robert was around his own children, and all the children in the parish. He's outraged and angry.

"We haven't seen Robert for weeks. No one knew what happened. He was just gone."

"That's what happened. The Archbishop removed him from all of his positions."

"Wow."

Dean shares the news with a few trusted friends. Other than a few dispatches from Dean, I have no idea what happens at the parish. I never return to it. I never speak to anyone else from it. The thought of that church is too painful. I let it all go, except for Dean. He is the one light that keeps shining in my life from that time.

88

The Criminal Case

Many months after the Orthodox Church has, in their own way, found Robert guilty, the Detroit Prosecutor's Office makes their case. It's been slow going. First, they have to find a reason, that isn't just Kamau's word against his, to arrest Robert. They find this on a stakeout, when a boy is found entering Robert's house, a violation of his sex offender status. Now able to issue a search warrant, the Prosecuting Attorney's Office sends police officers into Robert's place. They find over 200 images of young boys, mostly from the Dominican Republic, in his possession, but there is still nothing to link him to Kamau. This is frustrating, but they keep trying.

89

Testifying

The prosecutor is a young, fiery Middle-Eastern man. He calls me several times, and asks all about Kamau, his accident, and his state of mind. I tell him, and explain that Kamau still has some residue of the delusions that were fixed for so long in his mind. He has bouts of confusion. He may not do well if interrogated on the stand. The man explains that no one else is coming forward. If some evidence is found, and Kamau is needed to testify, he will be the sole victim's voice raised against Robert. I understand the challenge here.

I'm concerned for my boy. There is no way we can prepare him to testify so far away from Detroit. We will just have to see how it all plays out. I try to stay prayerful.

90

Confession

I'm in my pastor's office. He is an extraordinary biracial priest, part African American and part Filipino. He always says, "I got the fried chicken and the egg rolls!" Father Norman is one of the most dynamic people I know. He is young, a priest who is likely to break into a rap during his homily, and he is funny, but he's also gentle and kind, and generous. Today, I'm in confession in his office. I'm talking about how difficult it is to get past what Robert has done, and the damage he's caused.

"It affects my whole spiritual life. I just don't trust like I used to. I don't trust church. I don't trust God anymore. I want to, but I don't. I know I have to forgive Robert, and the church, and even God, but it's hard. I feel like I'm guarding my heart."

Father Norman listens. His brown eyes regard mine with tenderness. "Breathe in the Holy Spirit," he tells me.

I take in a deep breath full of God.

"Now breathe out unforgiveness and pain."

I try to exhale these troublesome emotions.

"Robert owes you a debt that he cannot repay. Forgive him. That's where you start."

Give us this day our daily bread, the Lord's prayer says. And forgive us our debts, as we forgive our debtors. I breathe in the knowledge that Robert owes me big time; I breathe out he cannot pay me back for what he's done. Forgive him.

God, I'm willing to forgive. I'm willing. Help me.

That's all I have. For now, it will have to do.

Father Norman absolves me of my sins. We pray together for justice for Kamau, and he gives me a simple penance. My sins are forgiven. I go with some measure of peace.

Claudia Love Mair

91

We Got Him

One afternoon I'm at work, and get a call from the prosecutor. "We got him," he says. They've found some evidence against Robert that links him to Kamau. A single, damning email, among thousands on his computer, sent years ago, reveals Robert attempting to bribe Kamau for explicit pictures. One, single email which the attorney describes as a needle in the haystack. "It's a miracle," he tells me.

"It sure is," I say.

92

Trial

When it is time for the trial, I cannot go. I find some thin excuse to send Ken, but the truth is, it is all so complicated for me. Robert was my friend. He was like a beloved, big brother. The homicidal anger I feel toward him is expected, but no one told me that I would feel grief, or that on occasion, I would even feel sorry for Robert.

How can this be? This man who hurt my son so terribly, how is it possible that some small part of me worries that as a man in his sixties, he will not fare well in prison, especially with a sex crime against a child on his head. The fact is, I loved Robert. Sure, I want to demolish him after what he did, but I also want to sit in front of him, tearful, and ask him, like a devastated sister, "Why did you do this thing?" I don't feel ready to face the man I believed would teach my son about God, something I didn't think his own father could do.

Ken tells me Kamau did okay on the stand. It was hard for him, but he muddled through it. Sometimes, he was confused. Sometimes, he was frustrated. "You could tell," Ken said. "But he did okay."

It was enough. It was a miracle really, that he could get up there and testify at all.

93

"What About Robert?"

When it's time for Robert to be sentenced, I find my courage to face him and go to Detroit with most of the family. It's mid-December, 2014 now. Cold bites through my thin Kentucky weather coat as Ken, Abbie, Aziza, Nia, and I wait in an endless line outside of the courthouse. Kamau chooses not to go with us on the trip. He is ready to let the whole matter go. When we finally make our way inside and rush into the courtroom where Robert will learn his fate, victim impact statements in hand, we learn that Robert has already been sentenced and taken away. I never see him. He was the first to go before the judge that day, while we were stuck in line, waiting to get through security.

Robert took a plea bargain and was sentenced to seven to twenty years, the maximum, for criminal sexual activities against a child. He has to serve a minimum of seven with no chance of parole, and then will go before a judge again, who will consider our victim impact statements, even though we were unable to give them in person. They will remain in his file. If the judge deems it necessary, he will do the remainder of his time.

Twenty years does not make up for Kamau's suffering, but it's a start. The prosecutor tells us that our priest knew about Robert's background as a child predator and still allowed him to serve on the altar. This priest assured me that a sex offender would be a good Godfather to my child. I think he believed that God had changed Robert. He was wrong about that.

94

Sometimes

Sometimes, I think of writing Robert, and asking why he hurt Kamau—why he hurt *us* the way he did, but I'm certain there is no answer that will satisfy me. Sometimes, I pray for him, the way one prays for one's enemy. Sometimes, I pray for him the way one prays for a friend, the kind one has lost and cannot forget.

95

How It Feels

When I return home I asked Kamau how it feels to know that Robert received the maximum sentence based on his courageous testimony. He replied, "It had to be done, and I'm happy to have done it. At least he won't be out there hurting kids anymore."

"It's an honor to know you, Kamau. You are the bravest person I know."

96

Marriage

Now that Kamau has stabilized, the thin threads that held my marriage with Ken together have snapped against the weight of the things of life: stress, change, desire for something new and different. Ken and I are not the same people we were when we got together. We no longer fit, if we ever did. He stays away from home more. With all the violence in the neighborhood, I don't blame him. I'm weary of it, too, but somebody has to stay with our family and help our girls feel something resembling safe.

After once again hearing shooting on the street behind ours, I decide I can do better. My dear friends, Elizabeth and Joe, have found themselves an apartment and there's a rare three bedroom available for rent, too. She doesn't ask me if I'm interested. She doesn't have to. I get the number and call the apartment manager. Soon, bad credit and all, the place is mine.

It's time for a talk with my husband. We meet before the move, before we even pack. It's just an ordinary afternoon when Ken comes to shower and change his clothes.

"This is the end of the road for us," I say.

"You're taking the apartment?"

"You better believe I am."

"Can I bring my stuff there?"

"You'll have to put it in storage. This is it."

Ken nods. "I wish you well."

"You, too, Ken."

I move out with my girls to a place where I don't hear shots fired when I lie in my bed at night. But I still don't feel safe.

97

Sometimes

Despite myself I have moments of startling joy. The kids and I, Abbie, Kamau, Nia, and ZZ, crowd into my Beetle like clowns in a tiny car. We are a circus, this bunch of mine, exploding in laughter and delightful chatter, and for a few moments there is something resembling happy in the midst of all the madness. I cherish these fleeting times when it seems like we are okay, and we are, despite everything, going to be okay.

98

And Sometimes

You go so long taking care of someone else, of everyone else, you realize much too late that you've forgotten to take care of yourself. Then you are a danger, especially to yourself.

99

Trigger

I no longer work at Good Sam. Now I work at a call center. I offer roadside assistance to customers of a popular rental car company. Ninety-six percent of the people who call are angry because something is wrong with their car. In the beginning I think I can soothe them. Near the end, I am the one needing to be soothed.

One night a customer calls with a typical complaint. She is at Universal Studios in Orlando. Her car won't start. After some troubleshooting questions, it's clear to me that she needs a jump-start. I tell her this, but she is angry. She is entitled. She is demanding. She is insulting. She laughs at my attempts to help her. I have had worse customers, but because I have been unraveling, because I am at the end of myself, I am triggered. Suddenly I am back to a time in which I was terribly abused, and I was her again, that small me, a battered, disempowered, mousy, small, and afraid girl. I rush off the call and cry at my desk. Then the fibromyalgia kicks in. My joints feel like they are locking. I beg to go home, hyperventilating and about to faint. Everyone stares at me.

I cannot go back to work the next day. Or the next. I feel smaller and less significant each day. By the third day I am nothing. I feel gravely depressed. I may as well not live. I pack my bag, badly, and drive myself to Good Sam, and plead with them to admit me. They refuse, citing that I used to work there. They would be biased. I cannot decide if this bias would be for or against me. It doesn't matter that I feel unsafe within myself. They discharge me from the Emergency Room without so much as a "Good luck!" I call Elizabeth so distraught that I cannot drive myself to another hospital. She arrives with her husband,

Joe, and they take me to a more welcoming place, some thirty miles away.

Stoner Creek Hospital is downtown in quaint, historic Paris, Kentucky. I should have been more specific when I told God I've always wanted to go to Paris, but the place is lovely. Even distressed I'm not completely immune to South Main Street's Victorian charm. Sunlight dapples the stately, old houses and businesses that loom just beyond the pastoral horse farms.

I'm admitted for suicidal depression. Elizabeth and Joe stay with me until I'm taken back to a place where I cannot hurt myself. When I unpack, I realize I have no shirts in my bag. I call Elizabeth and Joe, hysterical. They bring a supply to me so that I don't have to walk around the unit in the sleep jersey I'm wearing emblazoned with Beyoncé's words, "I woke up like this." I cry for three days straight in the safety of the hospital. That scream stuck in my throat is finally released as ceaseless sobs.

A rumor goes around the job that a bad call made me crack up. This isn't so. I was already full of cracks. It wouldn't have taken much to make me break. It could have been any random event that precipitated my emotional freefall, any old, seemingly harmless thing.

During intake and on several interviews I have with behavioral health nurses, doctors, and social workers, I describe that I feel like a broken pitcher: badly patched together, with whatever tribulations poured into me leaking out until finally, the weight of troubled waters shatters me. Lamentations gush out, and all I can think is, "I'm finished. It's all over now."

It's not over for me, however. In the week that I'm in Stoner Creek, they give me the tools—and the medication—to lift my head again. To inhale and exhale without feeling like there are razor blades in my lungs. I'd forgotten how to take a big, wondrous gulp of life, and then release it back into the world. Then repeat. Measured ins and outs, one breath at a time, until I don't have to remind myself to breathe anymore.

100

Sometimes

It's clear that the best thing you could have done, the bravest thing, was live. You stay alive because in the absence of any real certainty, your testimony of rising, stumbling through day, and settling into bed as night creeps across the horizon, is hope enough.

And if hope is a thing with feathers, sometimes you fly on it's back in the dark, in the general direction of a peace.

101

A Proper Ending

How does one find a proper ending to a story of catastrophe and beauty, of love and trouble? I chase the answer, but it flits as swift as a hummingbird, out of reach. To help me find my way I ask myself what is true about Kamau and me.

Here's what I know: once upon a time, my son, a brown, wingless, baby bird of a boy, took to the mournful air, flailed wildly down six stories, and failed to fly. When he finally hit the unforgiving pavement, it damn near killed us both.

Yet, we lived. Somehow, in the aching four years between the awful moment Kamau lifted his arms to split open the sky and the day I walked out of that mental hospital after an admission for my own troubles, we learned to take in the air and let it go again.

After I'm released, I need to see him. I know Kamau will understand what I've just been through.

I go to his studio apartment and find him outside. He's standing a few feet from his porch smoking a cigarette. He is tall, lean, and gorgeous in jeans and a powder blue T-shirt, and I'm taken aback by how good he looks. The child whose face was broken and resembled a jigsaw puzzle, the kid whose gap-toothed smile I grieved the loss of, stuns me anew.

I pull my Beetle into the parking space in front of his place, step out and nearly lunge at him. I throw my arms around his neck, and he reaches down and folds his arms around my waist.

"Maaaahmuuuh," he says in a silly singsong voice, "I luuuuve you."

"I went crazy."

He laughs. "That's okay. I do it all the time."

Now I pull away from him and look into his face. This time it's me who's uncertain. His toothless smile assures me, but I still ask, "We're going to be all right, aren't we?"

"I hope so!" Another laugh bursts out of him, this one more boisterous. In that laugh lives yes and no, and probably and maybe. That's all he has. It's real, and I take it.

I hug him again. We'll be all right, except for when we won't be. And then we will be. We live here, at the intersection of all right and not all right.

We hold hands standing in the parking lot, two crazy people who have somehow circumnavigated death, our feet firmly planted on the ground, neither of us ready to soar because we know that simply climbing the next step is hard enough.

I leave my boy and head back home. Somewhere between Harrodsburg Road and New Circle, I have my proper ending.

It's so simple, and it was there from the epigraph, in a snippet of a Langston Hughes poem from mother to son:

"Don't you fall now —
For I'se still goin', honey,
I'se still climbin',
And life for me ain't been no crystal stair."

Acknowledgements

I am profoundly grateful for my brave, beautiful son Kamau, who generously allowed me to tell his story. This memoir would still be churning inside me if Sena Jeter Naslund and Karen Mann had not created a community where dreams become real. Thank you. I will forever treasure my days steeped in learning in the Spalding University Low Residency MFA in Writing program. Deep gratitude for Kathleen Driskell, Katy Yocom, Ellyn Lichvar, and Jason Hill for their endless patience and support as I struggled through school. My mentors and workshop leaders, Roy Hoffman, Nancy McCabe, and Robin Lippincott shaped me into a better writer. I'm indebted to you. This memoir would never have found its proper form without the guidance and support of my brilliant mentor, Dianne Aprile. Elizabeth Burton, my residency wife and dear friend, has been my rock, along with Karyl Anne Fischer, Sara Beth Lowe, Kellie Carle, Lindsay Zibach, Lindsey Harris, Annie Crandell, Jessica Weisenfels and Bobby Harris. I can't thank you all enough for everything.

Thank you to my friends who always support me in every endeavor, but especially Lisa Joy Samson and Evette Drouillard Oatman. I also want to acknowledge what a tremendous affect Tim Farrington and his exquisite work has had on me. I'll always love you, Tim.

A heartfelt thanks to my family for putting up with me going away to school and spending so much time writing.

To my publisher. Tracey Michae'l Lewis-Giggetts, thank you for believing in me. Thank you for being my open door back in to publishing. We got this! An enthusiastic shout out to my editor, Shonell Bacon, you rock so hard I almost strained my neck to keep up.

I'd be remiss if I didn't mention my friends and work family at Good Samaritan Hospital. You are too many in number to name, but you all mean so much to me. I'm looking at you, Dr. Glaser! And finally, thank you God for so many miracles. You have given me amazing grace.

About the Author

Claudia Love Mair (formerly Claudia Mair Burney) is the author of the *Amanda Bell Brown Mysteries*, the *Exorsistah* series, and the Christy and Carol Award nominated *Zora and Nicky: A Novel in Black and White*. Her work has appeared on Beliefnet, Urban Ministries, and Dame Magazine websites, as well as in print in Discipleship Journal. When she is not writing, Claudia loves to paint and create mixed media collages. She teaches workshops on the creative process as often as she can. Claudia lives in Lexington, KY, with her three daughters and three crazy cats. Her sons are close by, and she loves the fact that all her babies are near. Claudia dreams of a creative life, where her passion for writing and visual art merge in service to others.

30448674R00096

Made in the USA
Lexington, KY
09 February 2019